SILVA SEMERCIYAN

Silva Semerciyan is an American playwright permanently settled in the UK. She won the William Saroyan Prize for Playwriting for her first full-length play, *Another Man's Son*, which was subsequently developed under commission to the National Theatre. Her other plays include *I and the Village* (Theatre503, 2015), *The Window* (Bristol Old Vic, 2014), *The Tinderbox* (Bristol Old Vic, 2014), *Gather Ye Rosebuds* (Theatre503, 2013) and *Flashes* (Young Vic, 2012). Her work has also been presented in readings and short-run productions by the National Theatre Studio, Birmingham Repertory Theatre, Nightingale Theatre, Adrienne Theatre, LA Theatre Company and Golden Thread Productions.

I and the Village was shortlisted for the Bruntwood Prize in 2011, and *Gather Ye Rosebuds* won Best New Play at the Brighton Fringe Festival in 2013. Her radio play *Varanasi* was shortlisted for a BBC Audio Drama Award. She has been a BBC Fellow at the Bristol Old Vic Theatre, a member of the Royal Court's Studio Writers' Group, and a writer on attachment at the National Theatre Studio. She holds an MPhil (B) in Playwriting from the University of Birmingham.

Other Plays for Young People to Perform from Nick Hern Books

Original Plays

100
Christopher Heimann,
Neil Monaghan, Diene Petterle

BLOOD AND ICE
Liz Lochhead

BOYS
Ella Hickson

BUNNY
Jack Thorne

BURYING YOUR BROTHER IN THE
PAVEMENT
Jack Thorne

CHRISTMAS IS MILES AWAY
Chloë Moss

COCKROACH
Sam Holcroft

THE DOMINO EFFECT
AND OTHER PLAYS
Fin Kennedy

DISCO PIGS
Enda Walsh

EIGHT
Ella Hickson

GIRLS LIKE THAT
Evan Placey

HOW TO DISAPPEAR COMPLETELY
AND NEVER BE FOUND
Fin Kennedy

I CAUGHT CRABS IN
WALBERSWICK
Joel Horwood

KINDERTRANSPORT
Diane Samuels

MOGADISHU
Vivienne Franzmann

MOTH
Declan Greene

THE MYSTAE
Nick Whitby

OVERSPILL
Ali Taylor

PRONOUN
Evan Placey

SAME
Deborah Bruce

THERE IS A WAR
Tom Basden

THE URBAN GIRL'S GUIDE TO
CAMPING AND OTHER PLAYS
Fin Kennedy

THE WARDROBE
Sam Holcroft

Adaptations

ANIMAL FARM
Ian Wooldridge
Adapted from George Orwell

ARABIAN NIGHTS
Dominic Cooke

BEAUTY AND THE BEAST
Laurence Boswell

CORAM BOY
Helen Edmundson
Adapted from Jamila Gavin

DAVID COPPERFIELD
Alastair Cording
Adapted from Charles Dickens

GREAT EXPECTATIONS
Nick Ormerod and Declan Donnellan
Adapted from Charles Dickens

HIS DARK MATERIALS
Nicholas Wright
Adapted from Philip Pullman

THE JUNGLE BOOK
Stuart Paterson
Adapted from Rudyard Kipling

KENSUKE'S KINGDOM
Stuart Paterson
Adapted from Michael Morpurgo

KES
Lawrence Till
Adapted from Barry Hines

THE LOTTIE PROJECT
Vicky Ireland
Adapted from Jacqueline Wilson

MIDNIGHT
Vicky Ireland
Adapted from Jacqueline Wilson

NOUGHTS & CROSSES
Dominic Cooke
Adapted from Malorie Blackman

THE RAILWAY CHILDREN
Mike Kenny
Adapted from E. Nesbit

SWALLOWS AND AMAZONS
Helen Edmundson and Neil Hannon
Adapted from Arthur Ransome

TO SIR, WITH LOVE
Ayub Khan-Din
Adapted from E.R Braithwaite

TREASURE ISLAND
Stuart Paterson
Adapted from Robert Louis Stevenson

WENDY & PETER PAN
Ella Hickson
Adapted from J.M. Barrie

THE WOLVES OF WILLOUGHBY
CHASE
Russ Tunney
Adapted from Joan Aiken

Silva Semerciyan

THE LIGHT BURNS BLUE

NICK HERN BOOKS
www.nickhernbooks.co.uk

TONIC THEATRE
www.tonictheatre.co.uk

A Nick Hern Book

The Light Burns Blue first published as a paperback original in Great Britain in 2015 by Nick Hern Books Limited, The Glasshouse, 49a Goldhawk Road, London W12 8QP, in association with Tonic Theatre

The Light Burns Blue copyright © 2015 Silva Semerciyan

Silva Semerciyan has asserted her right to be identified as the author of this work

Cover image by Kathy Barber, Bullet Creative, www.bulletcreative.com (Quarter-plate 'Cameo' camera image courtesy of National Media Museum/Science & Society Picture Library)

Designed and typeset by Nick Hern Books, London
Printed and bound in Great Britain by Mimeo Ltd, Huntingdon, Cambridgeshire PE29 6XX

A CIP catalogue record for this book is available from the British Library

ISBN   978 1 84842 502 6

Contents

THE LIGHT BURNS BLUE BY SILVA SEMERCIYAN

N
H
B

SECOND PERSON NARRATIVE BY JEMMA KENNEDY

N
H
B

THIS CHANGES EVERYTHING BY JOEL HORWOOD

N
H
B

PLATFORM

Commissioning and publishing a range of new plays for young actors which put girls and their stories centre stage is something I have wanted to do for a long time and, since Tonic Theatre was formed in 2011, it is an idea I have been looking to get off the ground. Tonic exists to support UK theatre to achieve greater gender equality in its workforces and its repertoires; essentially our mission is to catalyse a culture-shift in how theatre thinks and works, so that talented women are given the same levels of support and opportunity as talented men.

While it has pretty big aspirations, Tonic is a tiny organisation; we have one-and-a-bit members of staff, no core funding, and a very modest financial turnover. Because we have such limited funds and capacity, we have to use these wisely and consequently are extremely strategic about where we target our efforts. I spend much time looking to identify 'pressure points' – places where, with a bit of work, a far bigger ripple effect can be achieved. For this reason, much of our work to date has been focused on partnerships with some of the largest organisations in the country, because if they change, others will follow. But youth drama has always been clear to me as one of the greatest pressure points of all. It is the engine room of the theatre industry; tomorrow's theatre-makers (not to mention audience members) are to be found today in youth-theatre groups, university drama societies and school drama clubs all over the country.

If we can challenge their assumptions about the role of women's stories, voices, and ideas in drama, then change in the profession – in time – will be immeasurably easier to achieve.

Beyond this strategic interest in youth drama, I was convinced that girls were getting a raw deal and I found that troubling. Having worked previously as a youth-theatre director, I was familiar with the regular challenge of trying to find scripts that had adequate numbers of female roles for all the committed and talented girls that wanted to take part. In nearly all the various youth-drama groups I worked in across a five-year period, there were significantly more girls than boys. However, when it came to finding big-cast, age-appropriate plays for them to work on, I was constantly frustrated by how few there seemed to be that provided enough opportunity for the girls, its most loyal and committed participants. When looking at contemporary new writing for young actors to perform, one could be mistaken for thinking that youth drama was a predominantly male pursuit, rather than the other way round.

Aside from the practicalities of matching the number of roles to the number of girls in any one drama group, the nature of writing for female characters was something I struggled to get excited about. While there were some notable examples, often the writing for female characters seemed somewhat lacklustre. They tended to be characters at the periphery of the action rather than its heart, with far less to say and do than their male counterparts, and with a tendency towards being one-dimensional, rather than complex or vibrant, funny or surprising. Why was it that in the twenty-first century the *quality* as well as the *quantity* of roles being written for girls still seemed to lag behind those for boys so demonstrably?

Keen to check I wasn't just imagining this imbalance, Tonic conducted a nationwide research study looking into opportunities for girls in youth drama, focusing on the quantity *and* quality of roles available to them. The research was written up into a report, *Swimming in the shallow end*, and is published on the Tonic Theatre website. Not only did the research confirm my worst fears – more depressingly, it exceeded them. While many of the research participants were vocal about the social, artistic and emotional benefits that participation in youth-drama productions can have on a young person's life, so too were they – to quote the report – on 'the erosion to self-esteem, confidence and aspiration when these opportunities are repeatedly held out of reach... [and] for too many girls, this is the case'.

But despite the doom and gloom of the research findings, there remained an exciting proposition; to write stories that weren't currently being put on stage, and to foreground – rather than ignore – the experiences, achievements and world-view of young women, perhaps the group above all others in British society whose situation has altered so dramatically and excitingly over the past hundred or so years. Tonic commissioned writers I was most fascinated to see respond to the brief set to them: a large-cast play written specifically for performance by young actors, with mainly or entirely female casts and in which the female characters should be no less complex or challenging than the male characters. I asked them to write in such a way that these plays could be performed by young people anywhere in the country, and that there should be scope for every school, college and youth-theatre group performing the play to make a production their own.

At Tonic our hope is that the first Platform plays, of which this is one, will be just the beginning of a longer trajectory of work for us. Although it entails further fundraising mountains to climb, we plan to commission and publish more plays over future years. Our aspiration is that over time Platform will become a new canon of writing for young actors and one that puts girls and their lives centre stage. I dearly hope that they will be taken up by groups all over the country and performed for many years to come.

Lucy Kerbel
Director, Tonic Theatre

Acknowledgments

Tonic would like to extend its sincere thanks to:

Matt Applewhite, Tamara von Werthern, Jon Barton and all at Nick Hern Books. Moira Buffini, Kendall Masson, Matthew Poxon, Racheli Sternberg, Steph Weller. Arts Council England. The Austin and Hope Pilkington Trust. Anna Niland and the National Youth Theatre of Great Britain. Jennifer Tuckett and Central Saint Martins, Richard Williams and Drama Centre. The National Theatre Studio. English Touring Theatre.

To all the generous donors who have enabled Platform to happen. Above all to Joan Carr, who loved books, delighted in live performance, and who believed girls should never have anything less than boys.

TONIC
THEATRE

Tonic Theatre was created in 2011 as a way of supporting the theatre industry to achieve greater gender equality in its workforces and repertoires. Today, Tonic partners with leading theatre companies around the UK on a range of projects, schemes, and creative works. Our groundbreaking Advance programme (www.tonictheatre-advance.co.uk) saw us work with the artistic directors and senior creative staff of a cohort of England's most influential theatres to bring about concrete change within their own organisations and the wider industry. It is a process the *Guardian* commented 'could transform the theatrical landscape forever'. *100 Great Plays for Women*, our previous collaboration with Nick Hern Books, was published in 2013 to wide acclaim and was subsequently the inspiration for a series of lectures at the National Theatre. We are now delighted to be launching Platform, our range of new plays commissioned to increase opportunity and aspiration among girls and young women who take part in youth drama.

Tonic's approach involves getting to grips with the principles that lie beneath how our industry functions – our working methods, decision-making processes, and organisational structures – and identifying how, in their current form, these can create barriers. Once we have done that, we devise practical yet imaginative alternative approaches and work with our partners to trial and deliver them. Essentially, our goal is to equip our colleagues in UK theatre with the tools they need to ensure a greater level of female talent is able to rise to the top.

Tonic is Affiliate Company at the National Theatre Studio.

www.tonictheatre.co.uk

Nick Hern Books

Theatre publishers & performing rights agents

Here at the Performing Rights Department at Nick Hern Books, we're often asked 'Are there any plays for young people?'… 'Have you got anything for a large cast?'… and 'Is there anything with strong female roles?'

Whilst the answer to these questions is, in each case, a resounding 'Yes!' (and in fact the majority of plays we've published in the last five years have been *by* women), the number of plays that fulfil all three of these criteria – strong roles for a large, predominantly or all-female cast of young actors – is less plentiful. Yet that's where there's so much demand! Nearly every teacher and youth-theatre director in the country knows that it's girls who make up the majority of their casts, and yet the plays available are often dominated by men. Because we can generally only publish what is being produced on the professional stages of the UK, until the theatre industry starts staging more plays with these qualities, the numbers will remain low. It's a vicious circle.

So with Platform, we are delighted to publish and license three plays that give young women good, strong roles to get their teeth into, and that will help them build their self-esteem and confidence in their own skills.

Nick Hern Books look after the amateur performing rights to over a thousand plays, and we know from experience that when it comes to choosing the right play it can be confusing (and pricey) to read enough of what's out there until you know which play is right for you. This is why we send out approval copies: up to three plays at a time, for thirty days, after which they have to be paid for, or returned to us in mint condition and you just need to pay the postage. So there is no reason not to read all three Platform plays to see if they will suit your school, college or youth-theatre group. We're very hopeful that one of them will.

Performing rights to the three plays will be available at a specially reduced rate to enable even those on a very tight budget to perform them. Discounts are also available on cast sets of scripts; and the cover images on these books can be supplied, free of charge, for you to use on your poster.

If you have any questions about Platform, or any of the plays on our list, or want to talk about what you're looking for, we are always happy to speak with you. Call us on 020 8749 4953, or email us at rights@nickhernbooks.co.uk.

Tamara von Werthern
Performing Rights Manager
Nick Hern Books

www.nickhernbooks.co.uk

Introduction
Silva Semerciyan

Almost more exciting than achieving a goal is discovering a new way of working towards it. I came to this realisation in 2014 when, as the BBC Fellow at the Bristol Old Vic Theatre, I discovered that writers need not work in isolation. The project was *The Tinderbox*, an adaptation of the story by Hans Christian Andersen for the Bristol Old Vic Young Company. The director Lisa Gregan and I shared a fire for challenging assumptions about women, and the bland, almost catatonic princess of *The Tinderbox* was firmly in our sights for a major overhaul. By joining forces, both of us were expanding our practice: for Lisa, she would be including a writer in her already effective devising process; for me, I would be eliciting and capturing material through explorations in a rehearsal room. At first, we pursued these objectives almost independently, carefully planning ahead sessions and achieving measured results. But then, during the February half-term, when for the first time we were working whole days across a week, a kind of miracle seemed to happen. Pre-planning became less effective than thinking on our feet, right there in the moment. The material this produced was dynamic; it flowed from a mutual stream of consciousness; it had behind it the authority of artistic rigour, trial and error, analysis and final consensus. I came away from the experience feeling that there had been artistry in the process as much as the product. I longed to do it again. So when Lucy Kerbel of Tonic Theatre first broached the subject of a play for young people and asked me if it was feasible to write it in four months, I immediately pictured myself in a room with Lisa and the Young Company.

Long before we cast the play, we held initial research-and-development sessions with both the 15–16 and 16–24 age groups at the Bristol Old Vic. We explained the brief: to create a play with lots of great parts for girls, and the reasons new plays like this were needed. Lisa and I offered starter ideas for the company to test. Each one featured a woman from history that we both admired. As the groups were preparing their renditions of the stimuli, I had a chance for an offline chat with one of the male members of the Bristol Old Vic's graduate company, Made in Bristol. I put it to him – what kind of play about girls would you *actually* go to see? It was one thing to laud the aims of an initiative, quite another to travel from home and pay money to see the final piece. He thought a moment then said, 'I'd like to see girls robbing a bank or planning some other kind of heist.' A penny dropped. I realised that up until that moment, we'd been thinking of 'girl stories' in the sense of young women pushing against the patriarchy in one way or another. Many of the great women of the past fit this model, and so in a sense, their stories were all the same. In subsequent R&D sessions, the ideas I brought in were in a completely different vein. They were all about girls who had a plan, a plan that had nothing to do with being a girl – making a scientific breakthrough, hosting a rave, winning a war. At the last second, I decided to include the Cottingley Fairies, feeling quite sure that it would be dismissed as too girly, but there was something so appealing about the characters, locations, and enduring mystery, that I thought it just might stand a chance.

In mixed groups of boys and girls, we improvised scenes for each of these new ideas. It was immediately clear that the Cottingley Fairies were sparking limitless possibilities, whereas the other ideas kept fizzling out. The idea had legs – or in this case, wings. The reason for this may be that there were many similarities to a heist plot – Elsie Wright and Frances Griffiths pulled a fast one on the British public for over sixty years. In their story, there was a large dose of mischief and irreverence for the world events of the day. This in itself overturned stereotypes of girls better than any more plaintive appeal ever could. The Edwardians regarded childhood as sacred and strove to preserve innocence at all costs. What is wonderful in this story is that children seized their share of joy in a time of devastation, and perhaps that is what is most sacred about childhood. We see it in the smiling faces of child survivors of atrocities, in refugee camps, in slums, in circumstances that adults (rightly) find unendurable. Women are often told to put their feminist objectives on hold in deference to the 'higher' political concerns of the day. Mrs Pankhurst and the other suffragettes pressed pause on their own political aims to support the war effort and were rewarded with the right to vote. But Elsie Wright and Frances Griffiths did not put their childhoods on hold just because there was a war on. They behaved as children should behave – like children.

The rehearsal room for *The Light Burns Blue* was a joyous place to be. The cast were integral to the creative process, offering characters, dialogue, ideas for scenes, and continually pushing me to find more and more in Elsie Wright and Winifred Douglas, all with an unerring sense of both the comedic and the dramatic. They also contributed to the research process with each cast member pursuing a topic that Lisa and I set for them, among these were 'clairvoyants' and 'changelings'. One actor actually constructed a scale model of a Midg quarter-plate camera out of paper so that we could marvel at just how compact it was for its time. In my own research, I was astonished to find a quote from Elsie Wright's father, Arthur, in which he referred to her as 'bottom of the class'. It seemed an impossible designation for someone who could draw and paint so beautifully until I considered that in 1917 academic ability was measured by a much narrower set of criteria than we accept today. Howard Gardner's notion of 'multiple intelligences' would not enter the collective vocabulary until 1983; either a child could do their sums or they couldn't. This was an important discovery, made all the more poignant by the fact that 'soft subjects' like fine art and theatre have very recently been under threat – threat of funding cuts, marginalisation, and at the very least, derisive comments by policy-makers. It may be true that the UK must hold its own in an increasingly competitive world. It may be true that young women are more apt to drop science and maths in secondary school and that those with an aptitude for these subjects should be encouraged to pursue them; but the arts also deserve their place in the curriculum, as otherwise, in years to come, we will have to answer to the Elsie Wrights of this generation for overlooking their talent.

Sir Ken Robinson tells a moving story in his 2006 TED Talk about choreographer Gillian Lynne. In the 1930s, her school had written to her parents claiming she had a 'learning disorder'. Gillian's mother took her to see a specialist. After they had discussed the case, the doctor switched on the radio, and he and Mrs Lynne watched Gillian through a partly open door. Gillian immediately rose to her feet and began moving. The doctor advised Mrs Lynne to enrol her daughter in a dance class. She did so. Gillian Lynne went on to become the internationally famous choreographer of Andrew Lloyd Webber's *Cats*. Without question, Elsie Wright was artistically talented. The size of that talent is, to my mind, irrelevant. It was her defining characteristic, who she was. Today, we would think it abusive to stymie a child's one source of pride. How far she might have taken this gift if not for the fairies is impossible to say, but she achieved fame for dubious reasons. She was never recognised for her creations, even though her creations are amongst the most recognisable images in the public domain. The fixation with whether or not the fairies were real has overshadowed this achievement. I chose writing instead of science because I liked creating worlds in which I could control the outcomes. History should have made more of Elsie Wright's artistic ability. It has been a pleasure revising the record.

Acknowledgements

Lisa Gregan and the amazing and inspiring Bristol Old Vic Young Company who contributed everything from ideas to critique to fabulous lines of dialogue; Sharon Clark, James Peries, Siân Henderson, Lucy Hunt, James Kent and everyone at the Bristol Old Vic Theatre; Lucy Kerbel and Tonic Theatre; Jake Bright and Max Johns; Lizzie Philps, Nick Young and Michelle Hughes at SGS College; Dr Catherine Hindson at

Bristol University; Lily Williams at Curtis Brown; Matt
Applewhite and Tamara von Werthern at Nick Hern Books;
Moira Buffini; Bob and Marie Baker; my mother, father and
brother for their unfailing love and support, and David Caudery,
the photographer I know best.

Production Notes

The characters and events depicted in this story are fictions rooted in reality. There was an Elsie Wright who photographed fairies. There was a Frances Griffiths who posed with them. The photographs did manage to capture the imagination of Sir Arthur Conan Doyle, who did champion the photographs as proof that fairies exist. However, this is not a biography or a documentary. Nothing ruins a good tale like too much reality, and nothing demotivates a storyteller like the cold adherence to fact. The phrase 'poetic licence' is well-worn and often too liberally applied – at best, a conscious departure and at worst, an excuse. Something else is being aimed at here, and the Cottingley Fairies provided the starting point.

In the original production, staged at the Bristol Old Vic Theatre, AV slides were used to indicate the date or time of some scenes in order to orient the audience and prevent confusion. These appear in the text as 'optional slides'. Other methods are possible: simple placards could be used; alternatively, the actor who plays Polly Wright could speak the information. Any of these devices are optional.

The real Cottingley photographs were never presented on stage. Empty frames and blank photos were used instead as a stylistic choice: the audience had to work to create the photographs in their own minds from the clues laced throughout the play. This aesthetic extended to the set which presented a sketch of reality, including a forest of thin tree trunks with no branches or leaves. It also extended to the props, which included blank sketch pads to represent Elsie's drawings and blank sheets of A3 paper to represent newspapers.

Some scenes, e.g. '10. Legacies' and '12. Fairy Life', include descriptions of staging as they appeared in the Bristol Old Vic production. However, these sections may be interpreted and presented in a number of ways, and groups are encouraged to make them their own.

The original cast was asked to improvise white noise – that is, dialogue additional to the text, e.g. the murmurings of Londoners as they awaited the arrival of Elsie and Frances; the banter between the village girls. This helped to create a more natural overall effect. It was also a useful tool in transitions between some scenes where actors needed travelling time. For example, in '6. Village Art', the members of the art club entered from offstage already in the midst of an energetic discussion, none of which the audience necessarily tuned in to, and then the actors launched into the scene itself. These moments of improvisation should be judged carefully and used sparingly, so that they create a sense of life and vibrancy without ever working against the written text.

THE LIGHT BURNS BLUE

For Theadora,
who requested a play about fairies

Characters

ELSIE WRIGHT, *seventeen, the dreamer*
FRANCES GRIFFITHS, *Elsie's cousin, fifteen, the storyteller*
ARTHUR WRIGHT, *Elsie's father*
POLLY WRIGHT, *Elsie's mother*

GIRLS OF COTTINGLEY
all aged sixteen or seventeen
VIVIE, *the prankster, fun-loving, vivacious*
BETSY, *naive, sweet-natured, gentle*
MAGS, *the theorist, loves to read*
FLOSSIE, *the 'middle child' of the group, always feeling a bit left out*
JANET, *the pragmatist, a farmer's daughter*
AGATHA, *the dramatic one, a wannabe music-hall performer*

OTHERS OF COTTINGLEY
REVEREND COOPER
MRS COOPER
MR WYEDALE, *the baker*
MRS PEABODY, *a shopkeeper*
BOB, *a farmer*
BETSY'S MUM
MR BROWN, *an upright gentlemen*
MR TINDALL, *an elderly man*
MR DRAKE, *a photographer, Elsie's employer*
MR CATLING, *a local artist*
MR GAGE, *a local artist*
MRS BELL, *a local artist*
THOMAS, *a boy at Sunday school*
VARIOUS VILLAGERS *including a pub landlord, seamstresses and a fishing-net salesman*

EMPLOYEES OF *THE DISPATCH*
WINIFRED DOUGLAS, *a journalist*
LILLIAN CARTER, *the editor*
MARY WOOD, *a photographer*

ADDITIONAL CHARACTERS
MADAME BLAVATSKY, *a theosophist*
CLARENCE JOHNSON, *a clairvoyant*
SOLDIERS
CORRESPONDENTS
LONDONERS
THEOSOPHISTS

AND
SIR ARTHUR CONAN DOYLE, *author and dedicated
  spiritualist*

Setting

Cottingley, England

Although Cottingley is a real village in the North of England and would have its own dialect and regional accent, it is not necessary to present the play in authentic accents; this could be any village anywhere.

Optional slide: This story takes place in 1917 in a village in England called Cottingley, and in London.

1. Tableau

At a hotel in London. Saturday, 25 August 1917. 7.45 p.m. FRANCES stands on a raised platform, surrounded by picture frames.

FRANCES. We were playing. Down by the beck as usual when we heard voices. Singing. They weren't like human voices, more like the tinkling of bells. I thought it must be the wind or some of our friends playing a trick. But then we looked at the rushing stream, and there sitting on a rock was a fairy. We spoke to her, but she didn't reply. She waved her hand like to make us follow. And then… there they were. A little cluster of fairies, laughing and beckoning us. They made daisy chains and posies of harebells and laced campions and cowslips through our hair. We joined them in a dance. My cousin Elsie left me playing with them while she ran home to get her father's camera. When she came back, she took the first photo. She showed me how to use the camera, and then I took this one of her. She returned a few days later and took this one of the gnome. And then this one of the leaping fairy. And finally, this one of the fairies bathing in light.

SIR ARTHUR. Thank you, Frances. And now, ladies and gentlemen, I open the floor to your questions.

2. Before the Camera

Optional slide: April 1917.

The scene takes place in several locations across Cottingley.

At a church. REVEREND *and* MRS COOPER *are preparing for service.* VIVIE *bounds in.*

VIVIE. Reverend! Mrs Cooper!

REVEREND COOPER. Vivian, how are you?

VIVIE. I am WELL. And yourselves? How are your flock?

REVEREND COOPER. Oh! Well – haha! They're –

MRS COOPER (*sweetly*). Redeemable.

VIVIE. Well, you know what they say. A girl is raised by her village!

They all laugh. VIVIE *quickly continues.*

I have come here today to ask you just the teeniest tiniest little favour. Today is Elsie Wright's birthday.

REVEREND COOPER. Elsie Wright? Is she the one with brown hair?

VIVIE. Indeed she IS. What a great memory you have. Because it's Elsie's birthday and with all the sadness in the world, I was hoping we could bring a little bit of light to these dark times by baking Elsie a wonderful birthday cake.

MRS COOPER. What a nice thought, dear. Have you enough ingredients? Things are becoming scarce, you know.

VIVIE. That's just it. We have been scrimping and saving ingredients and we are nearly there, but you know what really makes a birthday cake a birthday cake? CANDLES. They're our way of showing our love to God, our love to the universe, and, God willing, our love to Elsie Wright.

REVEREND COOPER *withdraws one candle from a little bundle in his hands and begins to extend it to* VIVIE.

REVEREND COOPER. I'm sure one candle would be –

VIVIE (*quickly*). Seventeen? For seventeen years.

> REVEREND *and* MRS COOPER *look at each other.*
> REVEREND COOPER *hands* VIVIE *the whole bundle of candles.*

Thank you! Praise be to God.

At a bakery. MAGS *enters. Her voice is cheerful and pleasant but her face unsmiling and extremely matter-of-fact.*

MAGS. Hello, Mr Wyedale. I need some ingredients to bake a special cake.

MR WYEDALE. Well, Mags, you know we have a perfectly delicious selection of cakes in the bakery.

MAGS. No. This is a very specific type of cake. It's for Elsie Wright's birthday.

MR WYEDALE. Elsie Wright? I know. The one with the dreamy sort of yonderly face. I always make the mistake of looking where she's looking only she's not looking at anything.

MAGS. Yes, that is correct. May I have the ingredients, please?

MR WYEDALE. Well, er… do you have any money?

MAGS. No, I don't, but remember last week when I alphabetised your flour and yeast collections so you could bake your cakes very well? So I thought money wouldn't be important to you. I need equal parts flour, sugar, and butter, two eggs and a cherry.

MR WYEDALE. Why don't you go in the back and help yourself. Just let me know what you've taken afterwards.

> MAGS *is already heading towards the store room.*

MAGS. Thank you, Mr Wyedale.

At a shop. FLOSSIE *in a state of agitation, speaking to* MRS PEABODY, *lightning-fast.*

FLOSSIE. Arrrgh, I'm all in a flap. Right, I need some it's Elsie's birthday and my list my my list I need a card and er and some wrapping paper but the card – Elsie is SO particular about cards – oh dear, everyone is counting on me and if I get it wrong –

MRS PEABODY. It's all right, Flossie dear. Calm down. Just take it one step at a time, and tell me what you need.

At a farm. BOB *and* JANET *are rooted firmly to the ground, arms crossed, surveying stacks of hay bales.*

BOB. Hello, Janet.

JANET. Hello, Bob. You know last year when our farm gave your farm some extra hay?

Well it's Elsie Wright's birthday today, and we were needing some ham trimmings for sandwiches.

BOB. Oh aye. Which one's Elsie Wright?

JANET. Arthur Wright's daughter. (*Off his blank look.*) Down the lane, turn right, cross the ford, up the hill, last house on the left. A favour's a favour, Bob.

BOB (*grudgingly*). Favour's a favour.

At BETSY*'s house.* BETSY'S MUM *is whisking in a bowl.* BETSY *approaches quietly.*

BETSY. Mum… you know Elsie? Well, it's her birthday and everyone's trying to gather ingredients.

BETSY'S MUM. Oh, Betsy, you know your aunt is coming from Bradford tomorrow.

BETSY. I know, Mum, but I was wondering if we had… an egg? Just one?

It's just Elsie gave me her Eccles cake last month when I sprained my ankle.

BETSY'S MUM. It means a lot to you?

BETSY. Yes.

BETSY'S MUM *gives her an egg.* BETSY *smiles.*

Thanks, Mum.

She kisses her.

On the village common.

MR BROWN. Agatha?

AGATHA. Mr Brown! I have a particular predicament, Mr Brown. Mr Brown, you know Elsie Wright, don't you? Lovely girl, surprised everyone last month by putting her entire fist in her mouth. Well, me and the girls want to bake her a birthday cake, and I've lost my chocolate bar. It's just gone! So I was wondering if I could borrow a bit of yours?

She has already wrestled the chocolate out of his hands. She rushes off.

On the high street. The girls are all in a cluster and they have zeroed in on an elderly man.

VIVIE. Mr Tindall!

MR TINDALL. Hello, Vivie, Flossie… And who's this? I've not seen her before.

MAGS. This is Elsie's cousin, Frances. She's here from South Africa.

MR TINDALL. Well I never. South Africa! What brings you to Cottingley, lass?

FRANCES. My father's at war, and my mother wanted to be nearer to Auntie Polly.

MR TINDALL. Oh, I see, I see. What's South Africa like, then? Is it hot?

FRANCES. Oh yes. Ever so hot.

MR TINDALL. I expect you see all manner of animals, do you. Lions and such like.

FRANCES. Oh yes! This one time, a lion crept into our house and attacked our dog, Nimble. I had to beat him away with a broken-off piano leg. Another time, there was a giraffe with a poorly foot and I had to mend it with my mother's best shawl and –

VIVIE *nudges* FRANCES *to be quiet.*

VIVIE. Mr Tindall, today is Elsie Wright's birthday, and EVERYONE in the village has contributed toward a special party for her. You see, we all wanted to cheer her up because of her brother.

MR TINDALL. Elsie Wright... I remember! She's the lass won the cheese-rolling race last summer.

VIVIE. Not quite.

MAGS. She *likes* cheese.

VIVIE. We felt sure that YOU would want to do your part.

MR TINDALL. Well, yes of course, if it's not too... hehehe, well. What do you need from me?

VIVIE. Tea.

The birthday party. ELSIE *before a cake, beaming. The girls sing a song of congratulation appropriate to a birthday.*

ELSIE *blows out the candles.*

3. The Negative

Optional slide: August 1917.

Saturday, 25 August 1917. 7.50 p.m. At a hotel. ELSIE *is standing on a raised platform.* WINIFRED *stands below her, dressed in the professional skirt and blouse of a journalist.* WINIFRED *withdraws a camera from her satchel and points it at* ELSIE.

WINIFRED. Smile, Elsie.

> *She takes the photograph.*

ELSIE. It's you.

> ELSIE *stares at* WINIFRED *in disbelief.*

> I can't believe it. What are you doing here? And why are you dressed like that?

WINIFRED. I'm here in my official capacity.

ELSIE. Your official capacity? What does that mean?

WINIFRED. I mean my own particular –

ELSIE. I know what official means. Why did you leave like that? So suddenly? We looked everywhere for you. We even asked Constable Warren to help us. He said, 'What's one missing girl when there are millions of missing men.' And now, here you are.

WINIFRED. I know how you did it, Elsie.

ELSIE. Did what?

WINIFRED. The photographs.

> *A pause.*

ELSIE. Winifred? Is that even your name?

WINIFRED. Yes.

ELSIE. I thought you were my friend.

WINIFRED. Another person would have done this long ago.

ELSIE. Done what? What are you going to do?

A pause.

WINIFRED. I want you to tell them the truth. The people here tonight. Sir Arthur Conan Doyle. Your followers. As soon as they return.

ELSIE. What business is it of yours?

WINIFRED. I'm a journalist for a newspaper called *The Dispatch*.

ELSIE. A *journalist*?

WINIFRED. My editor has instructed me to denounce you as a hoax and report back on the reaction of the other guests.

ELSIE (*taken aback*). You wouldn't do that, would you? All the girls are here – Vivie, Flossie, Mags – even Viv's mum. It's our first ever trip to London. Please don't spoil it for them. My mother has never been so happy.

WINIFRED. You're not. Happy. Are you?

ELSIE. You don't speak for me. You don't know me. You were in Cottingley for two days and then disappeared without a trace.

WINIFRED. You'll tell everyone the truth because you *want* to tell them. You are going to stop this before it goes any further.

ELSIE. You lied to me. Now if you'll excuse me, I'm going to the lobby to wait for the others.

ELSIE *begins to go out.* WINIFRED *moves towards her and speaks with urgency.*

WINIFRED. Elsie, in less than an hour, reporters from all the major London newspapers are going to descend on this hotel. They will have one purpose – to learn the truth of the Cottingley Fairies. My editor wanted a major press event to launch the story. Of course, we'll be first to go to print – most of the story is finished. It only remains for me to describe the outcome of our discussion tonight.

ELSIE. What discussion? There is not going to be any discussion. You've obviously made up your mind. There's nothing more to say.

ELSIE *begins to go off again.*

WINIFRED. Wait. Elsie, wait. My editor wants a story. She's sure you're a fraud, but she's never met you. I have. And it's not as easy for me… because I saw something last month that made me think there was more to this than I first believed.

ELSIE. What? What is there?

WINIFRED. You told me yourself it's your dream to go to art school. The truth about the fairies *will* be revealed tonight. But if you convince me that you are an artist and not a fraud, I will defend you – against the world if necessary. If you don't, I will be the first to tear you down.

4. Momento Mori

Optional slide: March 1917.

At a post-mortem photography studio. ELSIE*'s dead brother, Michael, and her parents,* POLLY *and* ARTHUR, *are about to be artificially posed for a photograph. Michael has been dressed in his soldier's uniform. This is* ELSIE*'s place of employment, so she is serving in her capacity as assistant to the photographer,* MR DRAKE. *He hands* ELSIE *a metal contraption for propping her brother up into a sitting position. She nearly drops it.*

MR DRAKE (*sharply*). Careful. And when you're finished with it, please smooth out the backdrop.

ELSIE *positions the contraption. She sees to the backdrop.* MR DRAKE *adjusts* ELSIE*'s brother and locks him into place. He works on the face. He stops.*

It's no good, I can't keep the eyes open. (*To* POLLY *and* ARTHUR.) Do I have your permission to do something a little unorthodox?

POLLY *looks to* ARTHUR.

POLLY. Will it be respectable?

MR DRAKE. Of course. I am merely going to propose that we paint pupils on the eyelids. You won't be able to detect this artifice in the final photograph.

POLLY. Well, yes. If it will make him look more… [alive.]

She starts to cry.

ARTHUR. Please don't spoil your countenance, dear. This is for us to remember him by.

MR DRAKE *hands* ELSIE *a paintbrush and some paint.*

MR DRAKE. Elsie, would you mind? You're fairly deft with the paintbrush.

ELSIE *paints pupils onto her brother's closed eyelids.*

(*To* POLLY.) Might I ask how old your son was?

POLLY. Nineteen. He was wounded in the Battle of the Somme. He was beginning to recover when he fell ill with influenza. It took him so fast…

MR DRAKE. I'm terribly sorry for your loss.

ELSIE *takes a step back, finished with her brushwork.*

POLLY (*distressed*). It doesn't look real.

MR DRAKE. I assure you it will look real in the final image. Are we ready?

POLLY *and* ARTHUR *move to stand on either side of their son.*

(*To* ARTHUR.) If you don't mind, would you stand immediately behind him and hold his head in place…

ARTHUR *obliges;* POLLY *follows.*

MR DRAKE. Thank you for assisting, Elsie. I know it can't have been easy today, with your own family. Now, would you please kneel beside your brother and lean against his legs.

ELSIE *kneels beside her brother, in front of* POLLY. POLLY *leans down and kisses her.*

On the count of three. One… two… three…

Click.

5. Wisps

Optional slide: July 1917.

Thursday, 5 July 1917. 4.30 p.m. The village girls are lying on the ground, propping their legs up into the air. Their skirts have peeled downward to reveal the undergarments of the day. They continually make adjustments, trying to lift their bodies higher for a better perspective. MAGS *sits apart reading a book.* FLOSSIE *runs in, finally catching up with them. She stops.*

FLOSSIE. What on earth are you *doing*?

VIVIE. We're standing on the sky. The straighter your legs, the realer it looks.

MAGS. 'More real', I think you'll find, Viv. 'Realer' isn't a word.

JANET. Betsy, there's a hole in your knickers.

BETSY. There is not! Is there?

BETSY *drops back down in dismay and begins to hunt for the hole.* VIVIE *drops down, bored of the game. She leans towards the others excitedly.*

VIVIE. Hey! Let's play 'light as a feather, stiff as a board'!

BETSY. Oh, not that game. The vicar says it's occult. He says girls must be models of purity and respectability –

VIVIE. Oh, stuff that. Who wants to be the dead body?

FLOSSIE. Me!!!

VIVIE. Are you sure, Flossie, last time you wet yourself.

FLOSSIE. I did not! I've told you a hundred times, there was a natural spring!

FLOSSIE daintily lies down on her side and props her head up with her hand.

VIVIE. Not like that. On your back, obviously. You're a corpse.

FLOSSIE lies on her back.

Now, everybody kneel around the body. Hold your fingers like this and place them underneath her. And then we close our eyes and chant 'light as a feather, stiff as a board'. Eventually, she'll levitate in the air. Ready?

GIRLS. Light as a feather, stiff as a board.
Light as a feather, stiff as a board.
Light as a feather, stiff as a board.
Light as a feather, stiff as a board.

FLOSSIE's body begins to rise into the air. Soon, she is 'levitating'. Unable to bear it any longer, FLOSSIE suddenly screams.

FLOSSIE. Ahhhhhhh! Put me down, put me down!!!

They drop her down, bottom-first.

VIVIE. All right, you're down. Honestly, every time.

They all move away from FLOSSIE, grumbling complaints. VIVIE lies on her back and puts her hands behind her head.

AGATHA. Elsie, could I stay over? Mum's been crying again.

JANET. Did she get *the* letter?

AGATHA. No. Sometimes I wish she would get *the* letter.

BETSY. Aggie, you can't say that! He's your brother.

AGATHA. I know, but I can't help it. It's like she can't see anyone who's not in uniform.

MAGS. My mother is continually lighting candles for my father – highly irrational. The outcome of the war won't be determined by a bit of wax on a string.

ELSIE (*to* AGATHA). I'll ask Mother. I'm sure it'll be all right.

AGATHA (*casting a sidelong glance at* FRANCES). Can I share with you and Frances has the spare room?

FRANCES. No! Elsie's room is half mine now. I'm NOT sleeping in the spare room! It's haunted. One time I saw the ghost of a baby in a nightdress. Its face was all blue and its eyes were all bloodshot and its mouth was a terrible 'O' from how it had died screaming in agony –

She grabs FLOSSIE *suddenly who screams in fright*.

VIVIE. Which would you rather? Sleep in a haunted room or have to go on stage in only your knickers?

AGATHA. I'd rather go on stage in a top hat and tails like Vesta Tilley.

VIVIE. Come on, it's a game.

FLOSSIE. Go on stage. I hate ghosts.

MAGS. How can you hate ghosts?

ELSIE. I don't believe in any of that. Ghosts or witches or –

FRANCES. Angels. She doesn't even believe in angels.

BETSY. Don't you believe in God? The vicar will be very cross.

VIVIE (*laughing*). That's a good one! Very cross. (*Crosses herself*.)

AGATHA. Unicorns might exist – it's just horse, add horn.

VIVIE. Fairies definitely exist. Just look at all the things they do. Like when babies die in their cots. There's no other explanation for that. All right, here's one for you. Which would you rather? Have to eat liver and onions every day for eternity or eat poo once?

They all laugh in delighted disgust except FLOSSIE, *who rises and shouts in utter dismay.*

FLOSSIE. I don't want to do either of those things! (*Realising she finally has everyone's attention.*) I want to have a go at what you were doing before. Someone do it with me – Please? I'll feel silly doing it alone. Please? Come on, please?!!!

Some of the girls join her in raising their legs in the air to 'stand on the sky'. VIVIE *crawls over to* ELSIE, *who is still sketching. She tries to get behind her for a look.* ELSIE *clasps the sketch pad to her chest.*

VIVIE. What are you drawing?

FRANCES. She's always drawing. And when she's not drawing, she's TALKING about drawing which is almost worse. Uncle Arthur says that *really* clever people can articulate their ideas without seeing them – like the time I told him about my idea for a Yorkshire safari. Elsie thought it was a silly idea, but Aunt Polly said it was 'delightfully novel'. Of course, I am an expert in natural history and –

VIVIE (*firmly*). I *love* Elsie's drawings and paintings. (*To* ELSIE.) Go on. Let us have a look.

ELSIE *slowly turns the drawing toward* VIVIE. *We cannot see it.*

It's beautiful. (*To* AGATHA.) It's your granddad's hawk, Agatha.

AGATHA. Let me see.

VIVIE *shows her.*

Not bad. The tail's not quite right.

VIVIE. Mags, wasn't there a flyer outside the village hall saying something about an art exhibition?

MAGS. That's correct.

VIVIE (*to* ELSIE). You should submit something.

ELSIE. Oh no. I couldn't.

VIVIE. Why not? Maybe they'd put your drawings forward for a prize or for an expert to look at. Maybe they'd send them off. Where's good to send stuff to, Mags?

MAGS. An art school?

ELSIE *hugs* VIVIE *and kisses her cheek.*

ELSIE. I'll draw you next.

6. Village Art

Saturday, 7 July 1917. 11.30 a.m. At the Village Hall. A group of Cottingley artists congregate around a painting that we cannot see.

MR CATLING. It's just lovely, Mrs Bell. The brushwork. The colour. What colour is that, exactly?

MRS BELL. Rose.

MR CATLING. Yes, we know it is a rose, Mrs Bell. What colour of pink would you say that was?

MRS BELL. Rose-pink?

MR CATLING. Oh no, no, no. That's not a rose-pink. No. I would call that a salmon-pink. Like the ones that grow on the arbor outside the vicarage. Delightful. And this… so lovely. The contours. The textures. I could almost reach out and pluck one of those grapes, Mr Gage.

MR GAGE. Why, thank you, Mr Catling. It's not quite finished, but one does tire of painting grapes.

ELSIE *approaches with a portfolio.*

MR CATLING. Elsie, dear, the village fête is next Saturday.

ELSIE. I'm here for the art-club exhibition. I read on your flyer that any local painter can submit their work. I've brought my portfolio.

MR CATLING. Dear… the Cottingley Art Club is for more, shall we say, established painters. An artist needs maturity and knowledge of life in order to paint truly well.

ELSIE *takes out a drawing.* MRS BELL *lets out a gasp of surprise and delight.*

MRS BELL. Why, it's lovely. So lovely.

MR CATLING (*looks*). You have promise, dear, but I'm afraid there's no emotional depth to your work, no individual flair. Come back in a few years when you have experienced a few heartaches, a few triumphs. Perhaps the bittersweet joy of motherhood.

MR GAGE. To be fair, it is a dog.

MR CATLING. A great artist can make a dog look like a king.

MR CATLING *hands back* ELSIE*'s portfolio.*

Elsie, dear, why don't you and your friends go fishing at Cottingley Beck?

ELSIE *goes off, annoyed.*

7. Above Rubies

Sunday, 8 July 1917. 9 a.m. At Sunday school. The group is comprised entirely of girls except for one boy, THOMAS.

MRS COOPER. Thomas, if you will continue for us. The Book of Mark, chapter nine, verse twenty-three.

THOMAS (*relishing his own voice*). 'And Jesus said, if thou canst believe, all things are possible to him that believeth. And straightaway the father of the child cried out in tears, I believe, Lord. Help thou mine unbelief.'

AGATHA (*quickly*). I'll go next, Mrs Cooper.

MRS COOPER. Thank you, Agatha, but it's Elsie's turn.

ELSIE *looks to* AGATHA *with despair. She rises slowly, painfully.*

ELSIE. 'When. Jesus. Saw… that the people came… running… together… He… He… He re– . Re– .'

THOMAS. Rebuked.

MRS COOPER. I'll lead the lesson, Thomas. It's 'rebuked'. Elsie. Meaning, a 'sharp criticism.' Please continue.

ELSIE. 'Rebuked the fool. Foul. Rebuked the foul… spirit… saying into – unto – him…

Thou dumb and deaf. Though dumb and deaf…'

She can't go on. She is in tears.

MRS COOPER. No need to cry, dear. Flossie.

FLOSSIE. From where? (*Turns to* MAGS, *whispering*.) Where from? Do you know, I think I fell asleep for a second and –

MAGS *shows her.*

'Though dumb and deaf spirit, I charge thee, come out of him, and enter him no more.' (*Stops.*) Do you know, that sounds a bit odd, actually, when you think about it –

MRS COOPER. Margaret, please continue.

MAGS. I prefer 'Mags', Mrs Cooper. (*Reading perfunctorily at a brisk pace*.) 'And the spirit cried and rent him sore, and came out of him: and he was as one dead; insomuch that many said he is dead. But Jesus took him by the hand and lifted him up, and he arose.' (*Whispering to* FLOSSIE.) Highly implausible.

REVEREND COOPER *enters*.

REVEREND COOPER. Hello, Mrs Cooper. Are we ready for me?

MRS COOPER. Yes, vicar.

He moves to stand before the class.

REVEREND COOPER. Show me a girl of good character. Her price is far above rubies. Proverbs thirty-one, verse ten. A beautiful verse, but what does it mean? It means that no amount of material wealth can compensate for the loss of your good name. Your life must be as a portrait in which there are no censorable brushstrokes. No matter how perfect the rest of the painting, the eye is constantly led to the flaw. As you go forth from Cottingley, you take this canvas, this work-in-progress with you. Let it always be said of you: she was a credit to her village. And now, girls, please make your way in for the start of service.

THOMAS *puts his hand up to remind* REVEREND COOPER *that he is there, too*.

Oh! Sorry, Thomas, didn't see you there.

REVEREND COOPER *claps a hand on* THOMAS*'s shoulder and leads him out. The girls follow.* ELSIE *trails at the rear of the departing group*.

MRS COOPER. Elsie, would you remain a moment, please?

ELSIE *stops and returns*.

We've not seen very much of you this month. Is everything all right at home?

ELSIE. I've been… busy… Mrs Cooper, I probably won't be coming to Sunday school very much from now on.

MRS COOPER. Oh, don't say that, Elsie. I'll be so disappointed in you.

ELSIE. What's the good in coming? I can't understand a word of it. You see, I'm not in school any more. My parents agreed it was best.

MRS COOPER. Dear, not everyone is clever in the same way. You're quite artistic, aren't you. Your drawings are very sweet.

ELSIE. My drawings won't earn me the price of a pencil.

MRS COOPER. There are many religious paintings I could show you. *Madonna del Prato*, *The Tower of Babel*. Don't you want to know all about the great artists of the past?

ELSIE. Could I be a great artist?

MRS COOPER. Well, dear… that's a difficult question to answer. Ask yourself: does the world need artists right now? Or does it need nurses, teachers, land girls? By all means, keep it up as a hobby. Just look at my niece, Mabel. She's *so* clever with papercraft.

8. Models

Optional slide: August 1917.

Saturday, 25 August 1917. 8 p.m. At the hotel. WINIFRED *is jotting something down in her composition book.* ELSIE *watches her intently.*

ELSIE. Why are you doing this?

WINIFRED. I've never liked mysteries. When I don't understand a poem, I always want to contact the poet and demand an explanation. I've done it, too. Several poets. They always look utterly astonished to see me.

ELSIE. Why not read the poem and decide for yourself?

WINIFRED. I do. But I'm never satisfied that I have the definitive answer.

A pause.

ELSIE. Vivie will be really angry with you. She hates being tricked. And Betsy will be so hurt. And Flossie will probably panic and take to sleeping under the bed.

WINIFRED. Sometimes a journalist must go to certain lengths to uncover the truth.

ELSIE. So you're a journalist. That must be nice. Doing something useful. Something with meaning. People taking you seriously.

WINIFRED. I've worked hard to get to where I am.

ELSIE. Good for you.

WINIFRED. Let's discuss the fairies.

WINIFRED *shows* ELSIE *a copy of one of the photos.*

They're remarkably fashionable, aren't they? This one looks quite Parisienne.

ELSIE. I wouldn't know. Fashion isn't something people know about in Cottingley.

WINNIFRED. But you do get the ladies' magazines, the same as London or Paris.

ELSIE. I'm not allowed to buy ladies' magazines. My mother thinks they're full of nonsense.

WINIFRED. Have you heard of a book called *Princess Mary's Gift Book*? The illustrations are very similar to the fairies in your photographs. And you own a copy of the book.

ELSIE. No, I don't.

WINIFRED *withdraws a book from her satchel.*

WINIFRED. I took this off your bookshelf. (*Opens it.*) See this one here? She has her arms above her head. And this one is turning up and to the side.

ELSIE. I'm not a thief. I had seen those drawings but I didn't trace them. You won't find a single one of my fairies in that book. I never copy exactly because where's the fun in that? There's no challenge.

WINIFRED. No originality either. One could argue that altering an image only slightly is still largely an act of imitation. An artist is someone whom others imitate.

ELSIE. You're right. I'm not an artist. I don't have any training. My drawings and paintings rely on things I've seen, and they're of childish things like fairies and gnomes and elves. Now if you'll excuse me, I want to find Frances and my mother and tell them what's about to happen.

WINIFRED. Stop.

ELSIE *stops.*

When was the first time you used a camera?

9. Sparks

Sunday, 8 July 1917. 10 p.m. ARTHUR, ELSIE *and* FRANCES *are kneeling on the floor of the sitting room, all bent over the same magazine.* FRANCES *yawns long and loud.*

FRANCES. Ohhhh! I'm about to perish with exhaustion. I simply MUST retire to my room. Goodnight, Uncle Arthur. Night, Elsie.

ELSIE. Night.

> FRANCES *plods out of the room, demonstrating her tiredness with every step.* ELSIE *and* ARTHUR *look at each other and share a soft chuckle.* ARTHUR *turns the page of the magazine.*

ARTHUR. Look.

> ELSIE *leans in for a better view.*

Rather haunting, aren't they. They're also a deception. The photograph gives the impression that the soldiers climbed the hill of their own accord and the photographer simply happened along. But in truth, he asked the soldiers to climb the hill so he could take this photograph. Also, they're in silhouette. It is impossible to see their scars or their lice or even the expressions on their faces. In shadow, you can't see the disillusionment in a man's eyes.

ELSIE. They aren't disillusioned, Father. That's only what you see. Some things may get left out or changed, but a camera can't make up things that aren't there.

ARTHUR. That's right. The camera never lies, but people do.

> POLLY *enters.*

POLLY. Time for bed, Little Face.

ELSIE. Mum! PLEASE stop calling me Little Face.

POLLY. Why? There's no one here but us. I love your little face.

> *She takes* ELSIE'*s face in her hands and kisses her forehead.*

Off you go.

ELSIE *goes out*.

ARTHUR. Has she told you?

POLLY (*quickly*). Wait.

Satisfied that ELSIE *has gone, she nods*.

ARTHUR. She says she's not going back to Sunday school.

POLLY. What happened?

ELSIE *returns and listens*.

ARTHUR. She was asked to read. The hours I spent with her when she was little… I just can't understand why we couldn't get through to her.

POLLY. She's not stupid. Maybe we didn't start early enough.

ARTHUR. We did everything exactly the same as we did with Michael. It just didn't seem to take.

POLLY. There's no sense comparing them. They're very… He was very different.

ARTHUR. Are there any young men in the reckoning?

POLLY. There are no young men *around*. Even if there were, I fear they find Elsie a bit… unusual.

ARTHUR. I suppose there's the studio.

POLLY (*with a slight shudder*). It's such a gloomy place. A girl shouldn't spend her days propping up dead bodies for photographs. I could hardly stand being in that room for an hour. Arthur, why must she work at all? She's only seventeen. We're still here.

ARTHUR. She can't count on us for ever. How is her sewing?

POLLY. Not very good. Have you seen her drawings and paintings? They're wonderful.

ARTHUR. That's not a job. How is she going to earn a living? Mr Drake says he's prepared to take her on full time to assist him. He says he can't keep up with all the soldiers who need photographing. From next week, that's what she'll do.

ELSIE *is about to walk away. She stops. She knocks on the door.* ARTHUR *looks to* POLLY.

ARTHUR. Come in?

ELSIE *enters with an air of determination.*

ELSIE. Father. May I borrow your camera?

10. Legacies

The VILLAGERS *are staggered across the stage in various positions of stillness. The* SOLDIERS *enter and stand beside their family members, not touching them, facing forward at attention.*

SOLDIER 1. In the event of my death, I leave all my money and effects to my wife, Martha White, of 72 Lansdown Gardens, Cottingley.

SOLDIER 2. I, Henry Boot, leave all my money and belongings to my mother, Mrs Eliza Boot of 12 Bedford Lane, Cottingley.

SOLDIER 3. I, John Wedmore, leave all my money and properties to my father, Mr John Wedmore, of 45 Harwood Close, Cottingley.

SOLDIER 4. I, Mark Lewisham, leave all my effects to my mother, Gladys Lewisham of 87 Kensington Lane, Cottingley.

Through the following, the SOLDIERS *and their loved ones interact. All end in an embrace from which the* SOLDIERS *finally withdraw to retreat offstage.*

ALL SOLDIERS. Should I die in battle.
    If anything happens to me.
    If I don't make it home.
    If I die in this war.

The loved ones are left holding their legacies.

A WOMAN *holds a watch.*

A MAN *holds a pay book.*

A YOUNG WOMAN *holds a ring.*

A MAN *holds a fork.*

A GIRL *holds a hat.*

An ELDERLY WOMAN *holds a medal.*

A YOUNG WOMAN *holds a tin cup.*

AGATHA *moves to the centre of the stage, holding a photograph.*

ELSIE *goes to her and comforts her.*

11. Capture

Monday, 9 July 1917. 10 a.m. Beside the beck.

ELSIE. Frances. Hold still. Stop moving. Frances. A bit to the side. That's it. And now, ready, steady…

Click.

At home. ARTHUR *enters holding a developing tray.*

ARTHUR. Now then, Elsie. Let's see these photographs.

ARTHUR *places the developing tray down and lifts out a photograph.*

He squints at it.

He gives ELSIE *a look of irritation.*

He drops the photograph in annoyance, takes the camera from ELSIE *and goes out.*

ELSIE *stalks off, hurt.*

FRANCES *sneaks into the darkroom.*

She scoops up the photograph.

She gasps with delight and runs out.

Then in the village:

FRANCES *shows* VIVIE.

VIVIE *shows* MAGS.

MAGS *doesn't show anyone.*

VIVIE *gets it back off* MAGS *and shows* JANET.

JANET *shows* AGATHA.

AGATHA *shows* FLOSSIE.

FLOSSIE *shows* BETSY.

BETSY *shows it to her mother.*

Her mother shows it to POLLY.

POLLY *clutches it to her chest.*

12. Fairy Life

Wednesday, 11 July 1917. 8 p.m. At a Theosophical Society meeting. A row of THEOSOPHISTS *stand facing upstage, listening to* MADAME BLAVATSKY *and muttering words of approval as she speaks.* POLLY *is downstage, still clasping the photograph, watching them and working up the courage to approach* MADAME BLAVATSKY.

MADAME BLAVATSKY. And so in summary, fairies are associated with many things: death, life, nature. Their attributes have been documented in conflicting accounts across centuries. Are they protectors or thieves? Are they devious or merely playful? Whatever the answer, we theosophists believe that human beings are on course towards evolutionary perfection. Many people have claimed to see fairies, but only those of us nearest this perfection might one day tangibilise them at an opacity sufficient to make a mechanical record. Until that day comes, we live in hope. Thank you.

Applause. The THEOSOPHISTS *clink teacups against saucers and turn around to face* POLLY. *They lean towards her slightly and in unison sound an appraising 'Hmmmm.'* POLLY *tries to walk past them towards* MADAME BLAVATSKY, *but the* THEOSOPHISTS *lean to the side as one, and block her with another 'Hmmmmm.' She tries for the other side of the wall, they once again lean and block her with a 'Hmmmm.' Finally she tries to run past and is intercepted by a* THEOSOPHIST *at one extreme end of the wall who snatches the photograph out of her hands. The photograph is quickly passed down the line, each* THEOSOPHIST *looking and gasping in turn, until finally,* MADAME BLAVATSKY *sweeps forward and is the last to receive it.*

Who did you say you were again?

POLLY. Polly. Polly Wright.

MADAME BLAVATSKY. These photographs are extraordinary, darling. Just extraordinary. My followers will be overjoyed to learn of my discovery. So many are grieving, you know. The poor darlings look to me for solace.

POLLY. So you agree that they are real? My husband thinks they are childish nonsense.

MADAME BLAVATSKY. Of course they are REAL, darling. Just look at the expression on your daughter's face. She is beautiful, isn't she? Like a Pre-Raphaelite Guinevere. (*Looks at the other photograph.*) Your other daughter is quite charming, too, isn't she?

POLLY. That's my niece, Frances.

MADAME BLAVATSKY. I will cherish these photographs, darling. Cherish them.

POLLY. Madame Blavatsky, I have something to ask of you. There are those who are saying that my daughter is a liar. That there must be some fakery involved. Even her father says she must have drawn the fairies herself. But a mother knows her child. Elsie has never lied to me in her life. I was hoping you might be able to offer some expert insight to help me resolve this in my mind.

MADAME BLAVATSKY. Poor darling, you are clearly in a state of agitation. I can confirm that your husband is quite wrong. These fairies are as real as you or me. They have obviously chosen to appear in a form that would be most familiar and agreeable to your daughter.

POLLY. Can any being change its form? I've never heard that before.

MADAME BLAVATSKY (*sharply*). Obviously, there are a great many things you do not understand about supernatural phenomena. In cases like these, it is best to trust the opinion of one who has studied and written extensively on the subject.

POLLY. I beg your pardon. It's just that a girl's good name is so fragile and Elsie is on the brink of womanhood. I won't have people calling her a liar. Who would employ her? Who would marry her? I was hoping… Madame Blavatsky, would you please use your influence to publicise the truth?

MADAME BLAVATSKY. Of course I will, darling! What did you say your name was again?

POLLY. Polly. Polly Wright.

13. Seen

Thursday, 12 July 1917. A cluster of people at the centre of the stage holding newspapers. They adopt a pose.

READER 1. What? Photograph taken of a fairy? NO.

They shift to assume a new pose.

READER 2. *The Yorkshire Mirror*. Two innocent girls capture unholy spirits.

They shift to assume yet another pose.

READER 3. *The London Times*. Fairies invade Britain.

READER 4. *The New York Times*. Fairies influence British fashion.

FRENCH CORRESPONDENT. Fairies fly *en Angleterre*!

GERMAN CORRESPONDENT. Fairies used in the English war machine of MASS DESTRUCTION.

ROYAL CORRESPONDENT. King cancels Ascot to read about fairies.

A cluster of DANCERS assembled in tidy rows.

VILLAGER 1. And now! Join me in the latest dance craze that is sweeping the nation! It's called 'Don't Step On the Fairies!'

Music. The VILLAGERS perform the dance. Their bodies freeze.

VILLAGERS. I've been in the newspaper!

They disperse. Two VILLAGERS *move downstage and mime sewing.*

VILLAGER 2. I can't believe how well the business is doing!

VILLAGER 3. Girls.

VILLAGER 2. Just.

VILLAGER 3. Love.

VILLAGER 2. Fairy dresses!

A FAIRY GIRL *is hoisted into the air and carried, flying.*

FAIRY GIRL. I'm a fairy!

The VILLAGERS *gather upstage around the* PUB LANDLORD.

PUB LANDLORD. We've got our new selection of ales ready for you. Here we've got my personal favourite a light, sweet ale called 'Cottingley Fairies'.

VILLAGERS. Oooooooooh!

PUB LANDLORD. In the middle, we've got a dark, bitter ale called 'Fairies are Real'.

VILLAGERS. Ahhhhhhh!

PUB LANDLORD. And our final ale, which is not actually alcoholic. 'Fairy Milk'!

The VILLAGERS *applaud, then rush off and form a huddle downstage. Opposite, a* FISHING-NET SALESMAN *spiritlessly repeats his pitch over and over.*

FISHING-NET SALESMAN. Fishing nets. Get your fishing nets.

The VILLAGERS *murmur excitedly to one another, ignoring the* SALESMAN. *The word 'fairy' can be heard repeatedly amongst them as he continues his chant. He stops, looks at the huddle, considers.*

Fairy nets! Get your fairy nets!

The VILLAGERS *immediately turn and stampede towards him. They freeze.* MR CATLING *sweeps through them to take* ELSIE *by the arm and direct her towards the exhibition board in the village hall.*

MR CATLING. Elsie Wright, as I live and breathe! Come in, come in! Mrs Bell has kindly given up her space on the exhibition board to make way for your BEAUTIFUL photographs.

MRS COOPER takes ELSIE *by the arm and leads her into Sunday school.*

MRS COOPER. Today, class, instead of the lesson of David and Goliath, Elsie Wright is going to teach us how to use a camera. Thank you, Elsie! A round of applause, please, girls.

ELSIE smiles, almost smugly. THOMAS *puts his hand up to object to 'girls'.* MR DRAKE *intercepts* ELSIE *and guides her into his photo studio.*

MR DRAKE. If you think I'm going to fall at your feet, Elsie Wright, you've got another thing coming.

Beat.

Could I just get a quick photograph of you next to my mother?

An ELDERLY WOMAN *suddenly appears beside* ELSIE. *Click. A series of poses and clicks with the people of the village.* ELSIE *beams throughout, enjoying this elevation in her status.*

14. Grains

Optional slide: August 1917.

Saturday, 25 August 1917. 8.10 p.m. At the hotel.

WINIFRED. It was your idea. All yours.

ELSIE. All mine.

WINIFRED. And Frances went along with it.

ELSIE. Yes. She thought it would be good fun, but you know Frances. She isn't very patient. I had to beg her to sit still, practically forced her to do it in the end.

WINIFRED. Why? What was the… spark? Those first two photographs.

ELSIE. What was yours? What do you really want, Winifred? Is it money? Will this story make you famous?

WINIFRED. Fame isn't what motivates me.

ELSIE. What, then? Respect? From your newspaper, your readers?

WINIFRED. I suppose anyone undertaking a task hopes that if they do it well, there will be some acknowledgement. But to say that I was motivated by a desire to earn the respect of others wouldn't be accurate. I have to work to live. I chose this as my profession and I feel duty-bound –

ELSIE. Why? Why did you choose it?

WINIFRED. Well… if you must know… I read an article in a newspaper that made me angry and I wrote a letter to the editor refuting the article point by point. She contacted me and offered me a job.

ELSIE. Do you love what you do? Because I loved making the photographs. I loved the feeling of taking charge. Putting things in the frame, taking them out again. Writing with my eyes. If you don't feel that way about what you do… that's so sad.

WINIFRED. I love my job. I tell important stories of international significance.

ELSIE. This story? I'll wager you only got it because nobody else at your paper wanted it. (*Alluding to* WINIFRED*'s gender.*) Or was it because they thought you'd be grateful for anything?

WINIFRED. They underestimated it.

ELSIE. Did we make you angry? Is that why you wanted it?

WINIFRED. The idea of two spoiled girls wasting so many people's time, thumbing their noses at grief. I admit it did make me angry.

ELSIE (*a sudden thought*). Are you jealous?

15. Safelight

Friday, 20 July 1917. 2 p.m. At MARY WOOD*'s.* WINIFRED *knocks on a door. No answer. She knocks again. No answer. She gingerly tries the handle and opens the door a sliver.*

MARY. GET OUT! Don't you know any better than to barge into a blinkin' darkroom?!

WINIFRED. Sorry!

WINIFRED *pulls the door shut. She stands awkwardly, unsure what to do. She lamely knocks on the door.* MARY *emerges in a long smock, her hands stained with chemicals. She glares at* WINIFRED.

Are you Mary Wood? Lillian sent me. Lillian Carter. I understand that you are an occasional photographer for *The Dispatch*. I am the new reporter, Winifred Douglas. I'm investigating these fairy photographs that are all over the news at the moment.

An awkward pause.

I apologise for the intrusion. Have I spoilt anything?

MARY. No, fortunately. I have learned to shield my work against nitwits and reporters.

WINIFRED. You've seen the photographs, I suppose?

MARY. Yes.

WINIFRED. I was wondering what you thought of them.

MARY. They're a load of old codswallop, that's what I think.

WINIFRED. Yes, I know they're fake, but how? You must have some theory as to how the girls did it. From a technical point of view. Did they manipulate the image in the darkroom? Paint the fairies onto the negative?

MARY. Have you the original glass plates?

WINIFRED. Well, no, but –

MARY. Then I can't help you.

WINIFRED. I do have high-quality copies of the photographs.

MARY *gives her a withering look. She takes the photos and studies them. She hands them back.*

MARY. Without the negatives, I can't say for certain, but I see no immediate evidence of darkroom manipulation here. I'd say this is a faithful record of whatever was in front of the camera at the time.

WINIFRED. So the negative hasn't been doctored, it's that –

MARY. The fairies themselves are fake.

WINIFRED. How can we prove it?

MARY. That's your job.

WINIFRED (*looking at the photos*). They are pretty, I have to admit. The images…

MARY. What's prettiness good for? Allowing such foolish notions in children – how do we know what the results will be?

16. Overexposed

Friday, 20 July 1917. A series of letters. The
CORRESPONDENTS *take it in turn making their address.*

CORRESPONDENT 1. Dear Miss Wright, I am writing to
thank you for your wonderful photographs. At last, here is
proof, once and for all. Fairies DO exist.

CORRESPONDENT 2. Dear Elsie, I want to thank you for
giving me hope. They told me my son went missing in action
on the twenty-first of August of last year. I thought all
goodness in the world was gone until I saw your
photographs.

CORRESPONDENT 3. Dear Miss Wright, you can't know how
much your photographs mean to me. These are such sad
times, but you have given us all a cause for joy.

CORRESPONDENT 4. Yours sincerely, Evelyn Lewis.

CORRESPONDENT 5. Yours faithfully, AG Poole.

CORRESPONDENT 6. Warmly, Jesse Winters.

CORRESPONDENT 7. I look forward to hearing from you.

CORRESPONDENT 8. I very much look forward to hearing
from you.

CORRESPONDENT 9. At your earliest convenience.

CORRESPONDENT 10. PS We share a birthday.

CORRESPONDENT 11. Dear Miss Elsie Wright, I have seen
the wonderful pictures of the fairies which you and your
cousin Frances have taken, and I have not been so interested
for a long time. I will send you tomorrow one of my little
books for I am sure you are not too old to enjoy adventures. I
should like to hear all about it. With best wishes, yours
sincerely, Arthur Conan Doyle.

17. Shuttered

Friday, 20 July 1917. 4 p.m. At the office of The Dispatch. *There are journalists and others hard at work in a nearby space.*

WINIFRED. A thousand thanks, Lillian. You might have warned me.

LILLIAN. About what? Oh, you mean Mary? She's a kitten next to that lot in there. (*Indicates the other journalists.*) They drink hard, exchange ribald jokes and have ingénues like you for dinner.

WINIFRED. I can't get to the heart of this story by fiddling about with glass plates. *Why* did they do it? The only ones who can answer that are the girls themselves, but why would they tell me? There's nothing new to be said on this story, Lillian. With respect, I am capable of more than fairytales.

LILLIAN. Don't you know I've fed you the lead of the year – grown men chasing fairies in the woods? Women journalists are usually relegated to society luncheons and other tripe.

WINIFRED *is chastened by this.*

Now, I daresay the girls talk to somebody. Their friends. I am willing to give you a budget of ten pounds to use at your own discretion. In my experience, friends are changeable. And they hold each other cheap compared to all the things they're being deprived of in this war.

WINIFRED. You mean *bribe* the friends?

LILLIAN. Information is a commodity like anything else. Why shouldn't they be paid for it?

WINIFRED. The real scoop would be to get Elsie Wright to admit she's been lying. If only I could make myself invisible and watch them for a couple of days.

LILLIAN (*thinks*). You can. Be a girl.

WINIFRED. I beg your pardon?

LILLIAN. Put a ribbon in your hair, find one of your old dresses, and pretend to be a seventeen-year-old girl.

WINIFRED. That's… That would never work.

LILLIAN. Go to church one Sunday. Sit amongst the girls of the village so they can get a good look at you. Introduce yourself afterward. Even one day might be enough if you can get them to trust you.

WINIFRED. I'd never be able to pass myself off as a girl. I don't know any of the modern slang or what they're interested in. They'd see through me straight away.

LILLIAN. Blimey O'Reilly, you're only twenty-one. And you look like you're about twelve. (*Once again, pointing to the other journalists.*) You need to prove yourself to that lot and fast. They've all dragged themselves up through apprenticeships where they were badly treated. You wrote one brilliant article and waltzed in on a red carpet. But one article does not a career make. Show *me* you're someone to be reckoned with.

18. Dwellers at the Border

Sunday, 22 July 1917. 4 p.m. CLARENCE JOHNSON *leads a group of believers through the woods in search of the fairies. Amongst the group is* POLLY. *They arrive at the spot beside the beck where the photographs were taken. The village girls are nearby and observe everything he does.*

CLARENCE. Ladies and gentlemen, THIS is the very spot where the fairies first revealed themselves to Elsie and Frances.

He sniffs the air. The others sniff too, uncertain what they're sniffing for.

Ah yes… the phantasmagorical synergies are being transected by contrapuntal planes of existential phenomena. Close your eyes and connect with their aura. (*When everyone's eyes are shut, he quickly takes a swig from a hip flask.*) Some say fairies are the souls of our beloved dead returned to us on earth.

POLLY*'s face contorts in grief.* CLARENCE *seizes her arm.*

Yes, child, I see you truly believe. Have no fear, I shall summon the fairies with an ancient Sanskrit chant.

Namaste. Je m'appelle. Arrivederci.

Namaste. Je m'appelle. Arrivederci.

Namaste. Je m'appelle. Arrivederci.

Exasperated with his deception, VIVIE *steps forward.*

VIVIE. Open your eyes, everyone! You'll see the fairies a lot better with your eyes open!

CLARENCE. Pay no attention to her. Young girls are often jealous of fairies. Follow me to the next clearing. You will see fairies before this day is done, or my name isn't Clarence Johnson!

POLLY *and the believers follow him off.*

VIVIE. What an impostor! How can they fall for that? Poor Mrs Wright, what can she be thinking?

MAGS. I thought you believed in fairies, Viv.

VIVIE. Of course I do. But he's only been here two days. The fairies would speak to us before they spoke to a whopping great marrow like him. Mr Reece said he charged them all a pound to take part.

JANET *runs in excitedly.*

JANET. Girls! Have you heard the news? Elly and Fran have been invited to London by Sir Arthur Conan Doyle!

BETSY. Who's that?

VIVIE. Betsy, don't you ever read? He's the author of Sherlock Holmes.

BETSY. I don't like those stories. They always have dead people in them. Why can't stories ever be about kind people who get along?

JANET. There's more. He is going to pay for them to stay in a HOTEL.

AGATHA. A HOTEL! Oh, aren't they lucky! I'd LOVE to stay in a hotel! And go to Drury Lane and see a REAL show.

FLOSSIE. And get out of Cottingley!

VIVIE. We can, you know. All we have to do is catch one of the fairies.

FLOSSIE. Or maybe at least see one of them?

MAGS. Or say we did.

BETSY (*to* MAGS). We can't do that. The vicar says girls must be emblems of honesty and innocence.

VIVIE (*exasperated*). Oh, good grief, Betsy!

They all grumble disdain for the vicar's platitudes. Suddenly WINIFRED *approaches. The girls are pulled up short.*

WINIFRED. Hello…

VIVIE.…Hello.

She looks at the other girls. She scrutinises WINIFRED.

You're the new girl at church, aren't you?

WINIFRED. Yes. Winifred Douglas. We just moved here from London.

JANET. London, eh? Very posh.

WINIFRED. Not really. Not where I'm from anyway. (*Testing some slang.*) We had to scarper because we couldn't wangle the rent money.

MAGS. Your boots are made of high-quality leather and seem carefully made.

AGATHA. Where do you live, then?

WINIFRED. The old mill house – with my Auntie Lillian. Father died last month.

FLOSSIE. And your mum?

WINIFRED (*sadly*). When I was little. Sorry to bother you…

She turns and starts to walk off. VIVIE *looks to the other girls.*

VIVIE. Would you like to join us? We call ourselves 'the secret commonwealth'. Devotees of Queen Mirabelle, Fairy Queen of Cottingley. If you want to be one of us, you'll just have to perform a simple initiation.

BETSY. Oh, don't make her. With her mother and everything.

WINIFRED. No, no, I want to. What do I have to do?

VIVIE. You have to take the oath of honour and then jump across Cottingley Beck.

WINIFRED. I'm ready.

VIVIE. I… What's your name again?

WINIFRED. I, Winifred Douglas.

VIVIE. Will ever be.

WINIFRED. Will ever be.

VIVIE. True to the secret commonwealth.

WINIFRED. True to the secret commonwealth.

VIVIE. This I swear.

WINIFRED. This I swear.

VIVIE. Upon the soul of my mother.

WINIFRED. Upon… the soul of my mother.

FLOSSIE. Now jump!!!

WINIFRED *jumps across the beck.*

19. Hand of the Artist

Optional slide: August 1917.

Saturday, 25 August 1917. The hotel. 8.20 p.m.

WINIFRED. Now then, Elsie. Would you please draw me a fairy?

ELSIE. You've seen my drawings.

WINIFRED. I've never actually seen you draw. If you're tired of fairies, draw something else. Draw a flower.

ELSIE. I'm not going to *perform* for you.

WINIFRED. Your mother said you've always been artistic. But mothers have a way of inflating the truth about their children. My mother thought I could melt hearts with my singing and dancing but I was appalling at both.

ELSIE. When did you talk to my mother?

WINIFRED. That day at your house.

ELSIE. Why would I draw for you? You clearly mean to use the drawing against me.

A pause.

The next time I draw something.

WINIFRED. Yes, that's right. You'll give yourself away. To maintain this lie, you can never draw again. Your mother believes in you, Elsie. She says you're good enough to go for a scholarship to the art school in Leeds. Prove to me that you are.

ELSIE. All right. Here. I'll draw a fairy for you.

She takes the composition book and pen and draws crudely.

Here's the head and the body and the legs and the wings. There you are. There.

She thrusts the book at WINIFRED *and storms away.*

WINIFRED. You're not being very clever. I took the liberty of meeting with a man called Robert Carmichael, Head of

Admissions at the school. You may be an artist, but not the kind you think.

ELSIE. What kind am I?

WINIFRED. Mr Carmichael was uncertain. I asked if there was a case for considering the fairy photographs to be art. He said he would have to speak to you about your intention, but it was possible. I asked him whether you could, on that basis, be admitted as a student. He said yes. Imagine it, Elsie. You could go to the best art school in the north. And all you have to do is say that the fairies were your own creations.

ELSIE. I can't.

WINIFRED. Why not? Who are you protecting?

20. The Secret Commonwealth

Monday, 23 July 1917. 11 a.m. The girls with slingshots, running through the woods. VIVIE *leads the chase.* ELSIE *and* FRANCES *go along with it, to humour the others.* WINIFRED *struggles to keep up, she is less fit than in her teenage years.*

VIVIE. Was it just here, Elsie? I swear I saw something yesterday. A flash of light. Maybe we can pelt them out of hiding. Ready, aim, fire!

They all fire. FLOSSIE*'s slingshot backfires, and she hits herself.*

FLOSSIE. Ow! Why is it always ME?!

BETSY. Please can we stop looking? I'm so tired.

VIVIE. Don't give up yet! Did Joan of Arc give up? Has Mrs Pankhurst? I told you, we'll be famous for this!

JANET. Famous for killing a fairy.

MAGS. Indeed, yes. I still don't quite see the rationale behind the slingshots.

VIVIE. We aren't going to hurt them. We're just going to round them up. Come on!

WINIFRED. These fairies better be here or I *will* use this slingshot.

ELSIE overhears WINIFRED. *The other girls are starting to run off.*

ELSIE. Vivie, wait! Wait…

The girls wait.

I've… Listen. I've something to tell all of you.

She looks to FRANCES *who shakes her head.*

There's no such thing as a fairy. (*Off their looks.*) Fairies aren't real.

VIVIE. What do you mean? Of course they are. You photographed them.

ELSIE. We made them. I painted them with watercolours, then we cut them out, then we used hat pins to stick them in the ground. Tell her, Frances.

VIVIE *looks to* FRANCES. *She shrugs, but it's obvious she concedes.*

VIVIE. It's not true.

She looks to the others; they aren't as surprised.

(*To* ELSIE.) You're horrid.

ELSIE. I know how you feel, Vivie. I believed in the tooth fairy for a long time – then I found my baby teeth in the drawer of my mother's vanity table.

WINIFRED (*to* ELSIE). Are you implying that you made the fairies as some sort of contretemps –

FLOSSIE. Contre-what?

ELSIE. I had to tell you because you're my friends.

A pause. The news has hit VIVIE *very hard.*

VIVIE. So all the missing men… they really are missing. Aren't they?

She appears crushed.

ELSIE. I'm so sorry, Viv. I didn't know.

The girls all comfort VIVIE.

VIVIE. I never would have thought you had it in you, Elsie Wright.

ELSIE *hesitates, then withdraws a camera from her satchel.*

ELSIE. Sir Arthur Conan Doyle sent us this camera and asked us to photograph more fairies. He said he's going to publish an article about us in *The Strand Magazine*. And he's invited the London Theosophical Society to meet us at the hotel. I don't know what to do.

VIVIE. You should take the photos. He's a famous author. He must know your fairies are fake.

ELSIE. What would I say if people asked questions? I couldn't lie.

VIVIE. Just smile and let Sir Arthur do all the talking. You'd be a fool to miss the chance to see Buckingham Palace and St Paul's and Big Ben. They have it coming, if you ask me. They treat us like we're infants half the time.

ELSIE. But –

VIVIE. You'll be famous. Don't you understand what that means? It means the silly Cottingley Art Club can never turn you away again. Hang the Art Club – art *schools*, for goodness' sake.

A pause. ELSIE *is tempted by this.*

ELSIE. But how can we take more photos when there are always so many people around?

VIVIE *considers, then springs to action.*

VIVIE. Floss, you take stile. Mags, the hide. Betsy, you cover the entrance to the bridleway. Aggie and Janet, you cover the hay shed. Listen out for this. (*Whistles.*) Winnie, come with me. We can try to think of a way to get invited to London.

WINIFRED. No, I'll stay with Elsie and Frances. I can serve as the last wall of defence.

VIVIE *nods. As she walks off…*

VIVIE. Elsie. Never lie to me again.

The girls disperse. ELSIE *looks around her. She uses her hand to make a frame and looks through it. She positions* FRANCES. *As* FRANCES *tells her story, she keeps turning her head towards* WINIFRED. ELSIE *keeps adjusting it back into position. At last* ELSIE *moves opposite and kneels with the camera.*

FRANCES. I hope this doesn't take as long as the last time. I got so bored that I had to make up this whole story. Shall I tell it you, Winifred, you'll really like it. It was called 'Arabella and the Window Fairy'. There's this old jeweller's shop in the arcade in Harrogate and inside the window on a little perch lives the window fairy. She guards all the jewels in the cabinet. There are diamonds and rubies and sapphires and amethysts and garnets –

ELSIE. Frannie. Stop moving.

FRANCES *sulks.*

WINIFRED. Is this how you did it last time?

ELSIE. Not exactly. The Midg camera is older but less prone to distortion. Mr Drake says these Cameos have unbraced lens boards, so I'll have to hold it very still or the image will be blurry.

FRANCES. I'm BORED. How much longer is this going to take, Elsie?

ELSIE. Not long. (*As a gentle dig at* FRANCES.) I'm so glad you've come to Cottingley, Winifred. When I talk, you really seem to listen.

21. Double Exposure

Monday, 23 July 1917. 3 p.m. At the Wrights' house.
WINIFRED *has followed* ELSIE *home.* ELSIE *produces a pair of binoculars.*

ELSIE. Here they are. They're my granddad's from the Boer War. We'll be able to see any fairy hunters before they see us.

WINIFRED. That was clever – how you did the photographs. The fairy really seemed to be leaping at Frances. I'm sure you'll fool everyone. Why do you want to fool people, Elsie?

ELSIE. I don't.

WINIFRED. But you think they'll believe the fairies are real. Do you think most people are stupid and gullible?

ELSIE. No. Do you?

Unsure how to reply, WINIFRED *moves away. Through the following, she looks around, peeks in books.*

WINIFRED. It's so exciting that you'll get to go to London.

ELSIE. Scary.

WINIFRED. Because you're frightened of being found out?

ELSIE. It's such a big place, isn't it? And what if there's a Zeppelin raid?

WINIFRED. You don't have to go.

ELSIE. I don't see how I can refuse Sir Arthur Conan Doyle. Are you looking for something?

WINIFRED. No, no. I'm just admiring your bedroom. I wish I had a room like this.

ELSIE. What's yours like?

WINIFRED. I've never had a room of my own. There were so many of us. Never had a new dress in my life. I can mend a hem in twenty minutes flat.

ELSIE. I thought it was just you and your auntie.

WINIFRED. Oh… No… We were split up when my mother died. I'm surprised you don't display your drawings and paintings on the walls.

ELSIE. I keep them in here.

She goes to an old trunk and opens it. She shows WINIFRED *some of the artwork.*

Sometimes I tear them up. One time I made a bonfire of all my old paintings. Mother was so upset. She said I was punishing her because she had scolded me for getting my boots muddy. But that wasn't why I did it.

WINIFRED. Why did you?

ELSIE. They weren't perfect.

22. The Illustrious Elsie Wright

Tuesday, 24 July 1917. 10 a.m. The office of The Dispatch. WINIFRED *bursts in, in a state of agitation.*

LILLIAN. That was quick. Did you get the confession?

WINIFRED. I can't do this, Lillian. She's not merely a prankster. There's much more to it. She… There's something deliberate behind it.

LILLIAN. Deliberate nonsense.

WINIFRED. No, no, something more than that. She's showing us something about – *us* – the effect of the photographs on the people who look at them. Whatever the circumstances of the first photograph, when given the opportunity, she repeated the process in a very specific way. She might… she could be an artist.

LILLIAN. Not everyone who picks up a pencil is an artist. The fairies themselves are not original. The photographic composition is not unique. Above all, there was no meaning.

Ergo, it is not art. It's simply a practical joke to make her friends laugh.

WINIFRED. Listen. Until now, photographs have always been taken for fact. We don't question them like we do a drawing or a painting. A camera is a machine. It's meant to be incorruptible. With these photographs, the very objectivity of the camera is called into question. These photos may actually annihilate photography.

LILLIAN. So?

WINIFRED. So?! So she has gone from nought to the theoretical limits of an art form in half an hour. That's more than most people accomplish in a lifetime. Look at this photo. Look at her face. She's pretending to see the fairy. She's looking at her as if there is a silent understanding between them. What if Elsie knows something none of the rest of us know? That's often the way with artists.

LILLIAN. She's not an artist. Not by any accepted criteria of our time.

WINIFRED (*frustrated, half to herself*). How can I argue on her behalf when there are no words, no precedents, nothing to draw upon?

LILLIAN. Have you been taken in by this child for some sentimental reason of your own? I gave you a job at the paper because I saw something of myself in you. A fire to succeed. I sustained criticism for appointing you when you were clearly far less qualified than your male counterparts. Some called it nepotism. Some called it motherly instinct. My reputation rides on your performance. Either get this story or go be a governess and let me hire someone who's up to the job. For heaven's sake, she's a child, Winifred. Do maintain a sense of proportion.

WINIFRED. I'm not being irrational. And she's hardly a child. What will happen to her if she is publicly disgraced? The world never forgives a woman's mistakes.

LILLIAN. She'll be better off. A moment of shame, and then she can go back to being a child.

23. Perception

Optional slide: London, 2 p.m.

Saturday, 24 August 1917. 2 p.m. First day in London. Believers have convened on the hotel to await the arrival of ELSIE *and* FRANCES. *They are jostling for the best positions.*

LONDONER 1. I've been waiting for five hours. Kind of need the toilet now, though.

LONDONER 2. I'll hold your place for you.

LONDONER 1. Oh-hohoho! I'm not falling for that one!

POLLY, ELSIE *and* FRANCES *enter. A cluster of fans surrounds them, making it nearly impossible to walk. People continually shout 'Elsie!' and try to touch the girls.*

POLLY. Please don't touch them. Please leave her alone, you're scaring her.

A LONDON MAN *approaches* ELSIE, *cap in hand.*

LONDON MAN. Elsie Wright? You don't know who I am. But you've changed my life. Seeing something so pure in the world – I was a violent man. I know I was on the wrong path, but now I am back on the straight and narrow. Thank you, Elsie, thank you –

Two LONDON GIRLS *approach.*

LONDON GIRL 1. This is our scrapbook. It has every picture of you from the papers. It's for our brother.

LONDON GIRL 2. He's at war.

LONDON GIRL 1. But when he comes home from war, we'll show it to him, because he used to tell us stories about fairies when we were little.

LONDON GIRL 2. Sign my picture?

FRANCES *happily grabs the extended pen and signs the pictures.* FRANCES *whispers to* ELSIE, *excitedly.*

FRANCES. Elsie, look what we've done!

A LONDON MOTHER *approaches and takes* ELSIE*'s hands in hers.*

LONDON MOTHER. Elsie, I would just like to share with you that, thanks to you, I know my missing child is safe with the fairies. Please tell the fairies to send my baby back to me.

ELSIE *is shocked by this last entreaty. She hurries off;* FRANCES *and* POLLY *quickly follow after.*

24. Through Their Own Eyes

Optional slide: August 1917.

Saturday, 25 August 1917. 8.30 p.m. At the hotel.

ELSIE. Why have you waited? Why didn't you publish the story last month?

WINIFRED. I told you. I didn't have an ending.

ELSIE. You could have forced an ending. In Cottingley. You could have stood up in church. You could have invited the same newspapers.

A pause.

You don't want to do this, do you?

WINIFRED. I had certain reservations. I've made no secret of that. I will never publish a story if I can't stand behind every word of it.

ELSIE. You don't have to tell them anything at all. Silence is not a lie.

WINIFRED. What is silence in a burning building where others are asleep?

ELSIE. You could say you've made a mistake. You could say you were sceptical about the fairies, but after speaking with me, you see that you were wrong. You could help me get a place at the art school because you like me. Or have you decided I'm a fraud?

WINIFRED. I'm still uncertain. I need more information.

ELSIE. You don't trust yourself. That's why you write about other people. You need other people's thoughts and words because you have no opinions of your own.

WINIFRED (*bristling*). Let's face facts, Elsie. Your drawings and paintings are juvenile. It's the photographs – the way you behaved almost like an actress in them and the way they act upon the people who look at them. But *only* if you were conscious of what you were doing. Were you?

ELSIE (*challengingly*). What do *you* think?

25. Meeting of Minds

Optional slide: 3 p.m.

Saturday, 25 August 1917. 3 p.m. POLLY *leads* ELSIE *and* FRANCES *into one of the hotel's reception rooms where* SIR ARTHUR CONAN DOYLE *is seated, reading a newspaper. He rises and claps his hands together.*

SIR ARTHUR. Mrs Wright! Elsie! Frances! The pleasure is mine, truly. Do, please, have a seat.

As he returns to his chair, he spies a bag of sweets.

Oh! Girls, would you like a bit of rock? I'm excessively fond of a bit of rock. This was made by a sweet manufacturer in Covent Garden. (*Extends the bag.*) Taste?

ELSIE. No, thank you. I don't eat sweets any more, Sir Arthur.

FRANCES *snatches the bag.*

FRANCES. I do. Thank you, Sir Arthur.

SIR ARTHUR. Now, then. Suppose we get right down to the business at hand. I am not going to flatter you girls, and I hope you will always be honest with me. I had serious doubts at first. I am, as you may know, a scientific man –

FRANCES (*with candy in her mouth*). I thought you wrote detective stories.

POLLY (*admonishing*). Frances.

SIR ARTHUR. Yes, that is correct. But first I was a doctor – I only took up writing because I was having a ghastly time finding patients in Cornwall. (*Laughs. Stops laughing.*) The glass plates in the camera I sent you were all marked in order to detect any darkroom manipulation, but I am delighted to say there was none. Forgive my scepticism, girls. But when a man's reputation hangs in the balance, he must be very careful. Don't you agree?

ELSIE (*uneasily*). Yes, Sir Arthur.

FRANCES. Oh yes, Sir Arthur.

He hands them copies of magazines.

SIR ARTHUR. Mrs Wright, I hope you don't mind. I thought the girls might like signed copies of my article in *The Strand* with their wonderful photographs. (*To the girls.*) What was it like? Seeing the fairies up close?

FRANCES. It was wonderful, Sir Arthur. They were so beautiful. Exactly as I'd always dreamed. Their wings were like gossamer, almost the colour of the horizon on a cloudy day –

ELSIE *has nudged her to be silent.*

POLLY. Sir Arthur, I can't thank you enough for all you have done. It's meant the world to me that you've been so enthusiastic in your response. Even my husband has had to admit there must be something exceptional in the photographs for you to promote them as you have. In my life, I have experienced things that one might call 'paranormal' but until now, I always doubted my beliefs. I never felt I could share them with anyone.

SIR ARTHUR. Yes. People are quick to mock spiritualism and fairies. But rest assured, Mrs Wright, these photographs provide unequivocal proof that there is a world we cannot see. A world where the dead live again.

He holds up a photograph that we cannot see.

This was my son. Kingsley.

He struggles to compose himself. He turns to ELSIE *and* FRANCES.

Thank you, girls.

26. Two Village Kids

Optional slide: 4 p.m.

Saturday, 25 August 1917. 4 p.m. POLLY *and the girls enter a room in the hotel.*

POLLY. How lovely. I'll be right next door, girls. I want to finish replying to some of your letters.

ELSIE. Mum, you know you don't have to reply to all of them.

POLLY. Nonsense. I've never ignored a letter in my life. Besides, it's been wonderful discovering so many like-minded people. Don't you agree? (*With mock sternness.*) No jumping on the bed, Frances.

She goes out. FRANCES *immediately reacts with delight to their luxurious surroundings. She sits on the bed and bounces.* ELSIE*'s guilt rises at the sight of such splendour.*

FRANCES. Oh, Elsie, look. There are biscuits and everything. It's like being in a story! One for you, one for me. Two for you – (*Sotto.*) three for me. Have you ever been anywhere so wonderful in your life?

ELSIE. Yes, Wydale's bakery.

FRANCES. But these are London biscuits from a London bakery. (*Tastes*.) Ginger biscuits! And London sheets on the London bed. And look – lace curtains! And a view of the Thames.

FRANCES *looks out the window. She waves.*

ELSIE. Who are you waving to?

FRANCES. The people looking up at the window.

ELSIE. Which people?

ELSIE *goes to the window and looks. She backs away, shaking her head in disbelief.*

We have to tell Sir Arthur the truth.

FRANCES. Oh, please don't tell him. The hotel will throw us out and we'll have to walk home without coats on and we'll catch pneumonia and DIE and they won't let us be buried in the churchyard.

ELSIE. It would be a relief to get back to Cottingley. I hate all this attention. Don't you?

FRANCES (*lying*). Yes… Sir Arthur said we are to be the guests of honour at the gala dinner this evening. A gala dinner, Elsie! There's sure to be sorbet and everything. And all we have to do is wait until Sir Arthur has finished his speech and say the words we prepared. The girls are so looking forward to it. You can't disappoint them.

ELSIE. I have to. *We* have to, Frances. He's so kind, and he trusts us.

FRANCES. What about your mother? It's meant so much to her. You'll make her look silly. Not only in the village. They're already saying she's had out-of-body experiences and seen past lives.

A pause.

She'll never trust your word ever again.

27. Entourage

Optional slide: 4.30 p.m.

Saturday, 25 August 1917. 4.30 p.m. The village girls are in a hotel room. They are living it large. A cluster around FLOSSIE *on the phone to reception.*

VIVIE (*to* FLOSSIE). Quick, before Mum gets back!

FLOSSIE (*down the phone*). Ahoy… We are in room…

MAGS. Two-three-four.

FLOSSIE. Two-three-four. I would like to order some room service, please. We are here at the invitation of Sir Arthur Conan Doyle, so please send the bill of payment to him. We would like some chipped potatoes… and some…

AGATHA. Caviar.

FLOSSIE. And some caviar. And some…

BETSY. Chocolate humbugs.

FLOSSIE. Chocolate humbugs. Pardon? Sir Arthur Conan Doyle. Sherlock Holmes.

A knock at the door.

BETSY. It's your mum!

VIVIE. No, it's not. Mum wouldn't knock.

VIVIE *goes to answer the door. It is* WINIFRED.

Winnie?! Where've you been hiding yourself for the past month?

WINIFRED. May I come in?

VIVIE *looks to the other girls in surprise.*

VIVIE (*gently mocking* WINIFRED's *formality*). You may.

WINIFRED. Lovely room. How did you manage to garner an invitation?

JANET. 'Garner', eh? Very posh.

FLOSSIE. It was easy. We just told Sir Arthur that we had seen fairies KISSING.

VIVIE. What's going on, Win? Why'd you go off like that?

MAGS. And why are you dressed like a librarian?

WINIFRED. Girls, before I explain, I want to tell you that I already have much of the information I need, but there are still some missing pieces. If you help me, I will ensure that none of you are named in the article.

28. Nature

Optional slide: 7.45 p.m.

Saturday, 25 August 1917. 7.45 p.m. At the hotel. FRANCES *takes her place to form the same tableau as at the very beginning of the play. She is in the middle of her speech.* ELSIE *is nearby.*

FRANCES. When she came back, she took the first photo. She showed me how to use the camera, and then I took this one of her. She returned a few days later and took this one of the gnome. And then this one of the leaping fairy. And finally, this one of the fairies bathing in light.

SIR ARTHUR. Thank you, Frances. And now, ladies and gentlemen, I open the floor to your questions.

THEOSOPHIST 1. Did you touch any of them? What did they feel like?

THEOSOPHIST 2. What do they smell like?

THEOSOPHIST 3. Did you see any baby fairies? Or fairy births?!

SIR ARTHUR. As a matter of fact, the other Cottingley girls reported that they saw fairies engaged in a form of intimate embrace. That is, er, kissing. Isn't that true, girls?

VIVIE (*slightly sheepish*). Well, yes. That is, we thought they were fairies, but now we know they were only butterflies.

SIR ARTHUR (*annoyed*). An easy mistake, I'm sure. As regards the fairy births... Elsie, if I may.

He moves to point at one of the photographs.

As you can see, the gnome opposite Elsie has a navel on his abdomen. This, we may conclude, is evidence that fairies reproduce exactly as we do.

WINIFRED *rises.*

WINIFRED. Sir Arthur. Winifred Douglas. May I ask Miss Wright a question?

The village girls look at each other. VIVIE *quickly pushes past* WINIFRED *to claim centre stage; it is a planned distraction which clearly takes* WINIFRED *by surprise.*

VIVIE. Who would like to see the fairies?! Who would like to touch one?! They're right here in this hotel! I've seen them flying through the corridors! If you round a corner quickly enough, you can see them for yourselves!

FRANCES (*seizing her share of the attention*). Yes, that's right! Follow me! I'll lead you to them!

The believers run out in excitement. When ELSIE *and* WINIFRED *clock each other, we have now caught up in time to the moment of the first exchange between them.* WINIFRED *withdraws a camera from her satchel and points it at* ELSIE.

WINIFRED. Smile, Elsie.

She takes the photograph.

ELSIE. It's you.

29. Timed Exposure

Optional slide: 8.40 p.m.

At the hotel. We skip forward in time to the very end of the stand-off between WINIFRED *and* ELSIE.

ELSIE. Surely you have enough to go on, now. What more do you need from me?

WINIFRED. I know you have the habits of an artist, I know you have a passion for art, but I still don't know the fundamental reason why you created and photographed fairies. Why did you do it, Elsie? Why did you make the photographs?

ELSIE. I wanted to.

WINIFRED. People are saying that you're more evolved than the rest of us. I can't believe you enjoy it. You seem to me a very private person.

ELSIE. It's not about me, don't you understand? The photographs make so many people so happy.

WINIFRED. That wasn't your intention, though, was it.

ELSIE. What difference does it make what my intention was? Results are what count.

WINIFRED. I don't think you fully grasp what will happen to you if I name you a hoax. All those gentle believers outside will turn into an ugly mob.

Beat.

These people deserve to know the truth – if only to keep them from pinning their hopes to something that doesn't exist.

ELSIE. What good will that do?

WINIFRED. It will make them believe in the real world. You can stand at this podium and begin, 'I never meant to cause any harm…'

ELSIE. This will cause harm. Who are you to tell people what they should and shouldn't believe?

WINIFRED. It's time to set the record straight once and for all. The press will be here any minute.

ELSIE. Why would anyone want to be a journalist?

WINIFRED. It's freedom. To go where you want, pursue an idea to the end.

ELSIE. What was the article? The one that made you so angry?

WINIFRED. It was called 'What Girls are Good For'. It was essentially a treatise on why girls and women belong in the home. Written by some stale old windbag with three very unfortunate daughters.

ELSIE. You wanted to change something – not just for yourself but for other people. Have you forgotten that?

WINIFRED. Journalistic integrity means everything to me. More than any cause. Now tell me why you did it.

ELSIE. I've told you.

WINIFRED. No, you haven't. You've been playing. I want the reason.

ELSIE. There was no reason. Not the kind you're looking for. The night before I took the photos, I heard my father talking about me. I wanted to prove him wrong. But the next morning, I went into the kitchen and he was making toast and singing 'I'd Love to be a Monkey in a Zoo'. I wasn't angry any more. I thought, I'll make him smile. I'll make them both smile.

WINIFRED. But why fairies?

ELSIE. I believed in fairies for a very long time. I started painting them because I wanted to be able to see them. I photographed them because I wanted to make them look real. Because then I could pretend they *were* real. Because fairies are good. Are you satisfied that you have the 'definitive answer'?

A pause.

WINIFRED. How could you do it? There's a war on. How could you deceive vulnerable people? People are losing loved ones every day, including me. And you.

ELSIE. Don't – (*Recovers herself.*)

WINIFRED (*realises she's on to something*). You loved your brother very much, didn't you.

ELSIE. Goodbye, Winifred.

WINIFRED. You couldn't quite let him go.

ELSIE (*distress rising*). Please don't talk about him.

WINIFRED. There's something to do with your brother. Come on, Elsie, what? He died. He died and what? And then what? Tell me, Elsie, what about your brother?

ELSIE (*almost involuntarily, to stop* WINIFRED). Mother used to say that fairies were spirits of the dead. When I looked at the photographs, I could almost make myself believe.

A pause. ELSIE *is very upset, and* WINIFRED *suddenly sees her for the young, vulnerable girl she is. The sound of the crowd. They both start in surprise.* WINIFRED *goes to* ELSIE *and puts a sympathetic hand on her arm.*

WINIFRED. It's all right, Elsie. You can do this. I will help you.

ELSIE moves away decisively.

ELSIE (*impassioned*). No. I won't do it. The fairies *are* real. They are figments of my imagination, my thoughts. Can't you just accept that? We both know I'll never go to art school. These photographs are the only work of mine that people will ever see. I won't stand here and say they're fake, because that's like saying they have no meaning.

WINIFRED (*the eureka moment*). You're protecting the photographs.

The GUESTS *burst in, chattering excitedly. We can overhear one* WOMAN *say, 'I saw a fairy!' The* PRESS *floods in.*

WINIFRED *moves to the platform and shouts to gain their attention.*

Ladies and gentlemen! Ladies and gentlemen, members of the press!

A hush over the crowd, all wait expectantly.

My name is Winifred Douglas. I summoned you here tonight to hear the truth of the Cottingley fairies. A journalist is motivated by truth. The desire to make the unseen visible, to right the wrongs of others. The desire to finish a story well and leave no loose ends or unanswered questions.

WINIFRED *looks briefly to* ELSIE. *In her slight smile, we know that she has made up her mind not to denounce her. She turns back to the waiting crowd.*

The truth is this.

30. Image

The following text may be spoken by the actor who played POLLY *or may be divided among the rest of the cast.*

The entire photograph seems to glow from within. At the left of the frame, a glimpse of Cottingley Beck thundering down over rocks. At centre, Frances. Her hair hangs in long curls on either side of her face like a King Charles spaniel. There are flowers wreathing her forehead. Her face is serene, her gaze fixed forward, the faintest curve of a smile plays upon her lips. At the bottom of the frame, there is a bank of grass, and encircling her in a half-crescent, a garland of fairies. They all seem completely unaware of the attention they are receiving.

Optional slide: Five years before her death, Elsie, by then an elderly woman, made a public confession that the photographs were fake. Frances also admitted to having faked four of the five photographs. She maintained until her death that the fifth and final photograph was real.

A flash. ELSIE *is pointing her camera directly at us.*

The End.

The Light Burns Blue was first performed at the Bristol Old Vic, on 15 April 2015, with the following cast:

ELSIE WRIGHT	Kate Alhadeff
FRANCES GIFFITHS	Carys Patterson
VIVIE	Sydra Perryman
BETSY	Natalie MacHale
MAGS	Ruby Byrne
FLOSSIE	Amy Kennedy
AGATHA	Genevieve Sabherwal
JANET	Krista Matthews
WINIFRED DOUGLAS	Jenny Davies
LILLIAN CARTER	Elana Binysh
POLLY WRIGHT	Jess Clough
MRS COOPER/ LONDON MOTHER	Faye Bishop
MADAME BLAVATSKY/ MRS BELL/LONDON GIRL 1	Maisie Newman
MARY WOOD/BETSY'S MUM/ LONDON GIRL 2	Emily Rumble

ARTHUR WRIGHT/
    MR WYEDALE/
    FISHING-NET SALESMAN
	Josh Robinson

SIR ARTHUR CONAN DOYLE/ MR GAGE/MR TINDALL	Jack Orozco Morrison
CLARENCE JOHNSON/ MR CATLING	Dale Thrupp
REVEREND COOPER/ MICHAEL	William Bull
MR DRAKE/MR BROWN/ LONDON MAN	Scott Bayliss

BOB/THOMAS/
    PUB LANDLORD/
    LONDONER 1
	Hal Kelly

Director	Lisa Gregan
Designer	Max Johns
Musical Director	Jacob Bright
Lighting Designer	Owain Davies
Stage Manager	Cheryl Curley
Assistant Director	James D Kent
Assistant Stage Manager	James Dougherty
Assistants to the Designer	Ellie Roser, Zoe Brennan and Madeleine Caldwell
Senior Studio Technician	Jay Costello
Production Manager	David Harraway
Producer	Siân Henderson

www.nickhernbooks.co.uk

facebook.com/nickhernbooks

twitter.com/nickhernbooks